SCRIPTURE
AND TRADITION

Acadia Studies in Bible and Theology

Craig A. Evans and Lee Martin McDonald, Series Editors

The last two decades have witnessed dramatic developments in biblical and theological study. Full-time academics can scarcely keep up with fresh discoveries, recently published primary texts, ongoing archaeological work, new exegetical proposals, experiments in methods and hermeneutics, and innovative theological syntheses. For students and nonspecialists these developments are confusing and daunting. What has been needed is a series of succinct studies that assess these issues and present their findings in a way that students, pastors, laity, and nonspecialists will find accessible and rewarding. Acadia Studies in Bible and Theology, sponsored by Acadia Divinity College in Wolfville, Nova Scotia, and in conjunction with the college's Hayward Lectureship, constitutes such a series.

The Hayward Lectureship has brought to Acadia many distinguished scholars of Bible and theology, such as Sir Robin Barbour, John Bright, Leander Keck, Helmut Koester, Richard Longenecker, Martin Marty, Jaroslav Pelikan, Ian Rennie, James Sanders, and Eduard Schweizer. Acadia Studies in Bible and Theology reflect this rich heritage.

These studies are designed to guide readers through the ever more complicated maze of critical, interpretive, and theological discussion taking place today. But these studies are not introductory in nature; nor are they mere surveys. Written by leading authorities in the field, Acadia Studies in Bible and Theology offer critical assessments of the major issues that the church faces in the twenty-first century. Readers will gain the requisite orientation and fresh understanding of the important issues that will enable them to take part meaningfully in discussion and debate.

SCRIPTURE AND TRADITION

What the Bible Really Says

EDITH M. HUMPHREY

Baker Academic

a division of Baker Publishing Group
Grand Rapids, Michigan

© 2013 by Edith M. Humphrey

Published by Baker Academic
a division of Baker Publishing Group
P.O. Box 6287, Grand Rapids, MI 49516-6287
www.bakeracademic.com

Printed in the United States of America

Library of Congress Cataloging-in-Publication Data is on file at the Library of Congress, Washington, DC.

ISBN 978-0-8010-3983-6

13   14   15   16   17   18   19   7   6   5   4   3   2   1

For my friends at North Toronto Corps,
who taught me the infinite worth
of Scripture, and where I first started
asking questions about tradition.

CONTENTS

PREFACE

As I come to the conclusion of writing this book, I find myself enormously grateful for the many who have helped me, and continue to help me, to see the vibrancy of what has been given to the Church. "What do you have except that which you have received?" (1 Cor. 4:7 EH). In the context of this project, I especially am grateful for my husband Chris, who first challenged me to analyze what the Bible says about tradition—and whom I ignored until I had an inexplicably sleepless night when the question came back to haunt me. Thanks are also due to the kind invitation of Prof. Craig Evans, who hosted me when I delivered the Hayward Lectures at Acadia University in the fall of 2010, as well as for the forbearance and searching questions of those who attended these initial presentations, which formed the nucleus of this book. It is necessary also to mention the thought-provoking discussion that took place in the PCUSA Wee Kirk Conference near Pittsburgh, where I "tried out" these ideas in October 2010, and the keen interest of students who worked with me during my spring 2011 class on Scripture and Tradition at Pittsburgh Theological Seminary. For several years, too, I have been spurred on by conversations on this and related topics with three more-advanced students who have been discussion partners with me since their graduation from PTS—Matthew Bell, Timothy Becker, and Lisa Renée Sayre.

During the process of transformation from presentations to book, I have found invaluable the illuminating comments and gracious

suggestions of the Rev. Dr. John Breck, whose own work on Scripture and Tradition has been instructive to me (as to many others). I
hope that my volume will be accessible to the nonspecialist who is
interested in tradition—and this is a pressing concern to many in
the Church—without boring those for whom the topic is not new.
My assistant, Kathy Anderson, read all of this manuscript and was
invaluable in clarifying the prose and cleaning it up prior to its submission—no, Virginia, there were no ancient manuscripts found *in* the
Dead Sea! Further infelicitous details were discovered and suggestions
made by Alan J. Kirk, my meticulous colleague in New Testament;
Fr. Sean Taylor, my doughty comrade; and Bessie F. McEwan, my
ever-perceptive mother. Thanks also for the labor of friends at Baker
Academic, who partner with Acadia University in this series, and have
done further necessary work to bring all this to fruition. As January
draws to a close, I anticipate the Feast of the Presentation (Visitation)
at the Temple, and recall the wonder I experienced three years ago
when I first clearly envisioned holy Mary as the one who presented
herself to the Lord, and who offers the living Word to us, as she did to
Symeon: "Christ the coal of fire, whom holy Isaiah foresaw, now rests
in the arms of the Theotokos as in a pair of tongs, and He is given to
the elder" (Small Vespers); "Mary, you are the mystic Tongs, who has
conceived in your womb Christ the live Coal" (Matins, Canticle 9).

                                        Eve of the Feast of the Presentation 2012

INTRODUCTION

The Trouble with Tradition

Many people today have a love/hate relationship with tradition. Young people especially have gone beyond the twentieth-century love affair with all things "modern" and are beginning to feel wistful about lost family histories, forgotten ages, and remote times. In a rootless world, where millions live thousands of miles away from the home of their ancestors, and others do not even know where their forbears lived, many are turning again to historical fiction, in film or book, or rediscovering a love of genealogy. Family crests are reappearing, and advertisements at Christmastime speak with sentimentality about passing on (or even "creating") family traditions. But there remains a knee-jerk reaction, a disdain for what is old: without thinking, we often play off tradition against vibrant creativity. There are a few sayings about tradition (some of which may be seen as sign-offs in emails) that show our ambivalence:

- Tradition means giving votes to the most obscure of all classes, our ancestors. It is the democracy of the dead. Tradition refuses to submit to that arrogant oligarchy ["elite rulers"] who merely happen to be walking around. (G. K. Chesterton)
- Tradition does not mean that the living are dead, it means that the dead are living. (Harold MacMillan)

1

- We don't want tradition. We want to live in the present and the only history that is worth a tinker's dam is the history we make today. (Henry Ford)
- Tradition is an explanation for acting without thinking. (Gracie McGarvie)

Of course, debated matters are seldom simple. And so some have tried to explain the complexity of tradition and why we have opposing reactions to it. For example, we can distinguish between a healthy regard for the great people and the good things of our past, as contrasted with either an unthinking acceptance or a slavishness to all things antiquarian just because they are old. In making just such a distinction, the late Jaroslav Pelikan quipped: "Tradition is the living faith of the dead; traditionalism is the dead faith of the living."[1]

Even on a popular level, this tension for and against tradition is expressed. Ours is probably not the only family that was enchanted by the film adaptation of Scholem Aleichem's stories about Tevye and his daughters. (However, with three surprisingly different daughters, yet all of a romantic bent, perhaps the Humphrey household was particularly predisposed to a fixation upon the *Fiddler on the Roof*.)[2] In monologue and song, the engaging Tevye immortalizes the turmoil that can rage, even internally, within one person, as he or she tries to make important distinctions regarding received ways of living and thinking. Which are traditions that can be released, and which is *the* tradition, the internal DNA that makes up who we are, and without which we would be lost?

> A fiddler on the roof. Sounds crazy, no? But here, in our little village of Anatevka, you might say every one of us is a fiddler on the roof trying to scratch out a pleasant, simple tune without breaking his neck. It isn't easy. You may ask "Why do we stay up there if it's so dangerous?" Well, we stay because Anatevka is our home. And how do we keep

1. Pelikan, *The Vindication of Tradition*, 65.
2. It is a testimony to the depth of this popular musical that the mere mention of the word "tradition" evokes it in the contemporary imagination. Pelikan, on page 3 of *The Vindication of Tradition*, reminds us that for director Jerome Robbins, the development of the theme was key to the entire story: "If it's a show about tradition and its dissolution, then the audience should be told what that tradition is."

our balance? That I can tell you in one word: tradition! ... Traditions, traditions. Without our traditions our lives would be as shaky as, as ... as a fiddler on the roof![3]

Tevye is by nature a traditionalist, but he is forced to weigh matters as his customary life crumbles around him. The tradition of using a matchmaker to arrange marriages for his daughters is something that he can learn to forgo, though with reluctance. But traditional Judaism is a different matter: it is his true home, more solid even than the little town Anatevka that he will be forced to leave. Asked to accept his youngest daughter's marriage to a gentile, he exclaims, in torment: "If I try to bend that far, I will break!"

Tradition as a Pair of Glasses

No doubt some of us who consider these matters are, like Tevye, conservative in temperament—determined in this day of pell-mell change to conserve the treasures of the past. But even those of us who are oriented more toward the future need to understand the power and the meaning of tradition. Christians, by nature, with legitimacy can play it both ways—for we lay hold to a holy past but also look forward to God's promised future. We retain the Old Testament while living within the New Covenant forged by the Triune God. God's mercies are "new every morning" (Lam. 3:23). However, to stress the future at the expense of the past would be to lose what makes up our faith. As Jaroslav Pelikan so cogently argues in his own lecture, published as *The Vindication of Tradition*, even those who yearn for the disintegration of a certain tradition need to understand that tradition:

> [A] young audience should be told what that tradition is as a part of the record of its dissolution. For even if—or especially if—the tradition of our past is a burden that the next generation must finally drop, it will not be able to drop it, or to understand why it must drop it, unless it has some sense of what its content is and of how and why it has persisted for so long. The tradition does not have to be understood to

3. This quotation, taken from the opening and closing lines of Tevye's first appearance in the film, may be seen in the online collection of quotables at http://www .imdb.com/title/tt0067093/quotes. Accessed January 2012.

be dominant. . . . In fact, so long as the tradition is not understood, some parts of it, however transmuted they may be, can continue to be dominant.[4]

Pelikan's words, of course, are directed toward tradition in general and disclose to us why the "classics" of any culture need to be known and understood, even when (or perhaps *especially* when) a community is in the midst of upheaval and change. Those yearning for reform may not see that unacknowledged traditions stand at the foundation of what they are trying to reform—for good or for ill. Pelikan speaks about the recapturing of tradition as an exercise in "supplying the quotation marks."[5] My own generation of baby boomers and those that followed seem to be, by and large, unaware of the wide-scale amnesia that has taken hold—forgetfulness of the literary classics that have shaped our culture, near oblivion concerning moral and philosophical foundations, a casual ignorance concerning the sacred texts. Nearly twenty years ago, when I instructed Bible at the undergraduate level in Montreal, the McGill Religious Studies Department offered a biblical literacy course that was keenly sought out not only by humanities students but also by those pursuing music, law, and even science degrees. The literary buffs among the student body lamented that, though we could offer them remedial help (supply the quotation marks) so that they could recognize allusions to the Bible as they studied their texts, they would never have the "Aha!" experience common to those for whom the Bible was part of the air that they breathed. The crash course we offered them was helpful (symbolism, major characters of the Bible, historical timelines), but it was more like explaining a joke—intimate familiarity with a tradition is necessary for an immediate and deep appreciation of a work of art that is in continuity with, or even in reaction to, that tradition. Students of the 1980s and 1990s had been robbed of this past, and so of the pleasant experience of discovery and immediate recognition. The situation is even worse today. Many do not even know that they do not know.

Every year that I teach "Introduction to the New Testament" at seminary, I seek to demonstrate to candidates for ministry the extent

4. Pelikan, *The Vindication of Tradition*, 19.
5. Ibid., 4.

of this forgetfulness, for this malady has infected even those who seek leadership in the churches. I tell them the story of the 1940 battle at Dunkirk, when the allies were attempting to halt the German movement into France, and the British Expeditionary Force found itself trapped in a pincer movement, eventually completely isolated on the beaches of this French town. Waiting in what they assumed was the calm before the storm, the commander of the force sent a simple three-word message back to the home office—"But if not." At this point in telling the story, I pause and look expectantly at the incoming class. "So?" I ask. "What would this message have meant to you, had you received it?" Usually I am confronted by a sea of puzzled faces. Only twice in nine years has some keen student racked his or her brain and emerged with something like—"Oh, of course! He was referring to Daniel and the three young men who were facing the fiery furnace. Daniel defied the king, saying that the true God of Israel could deliver them, *but if not* they refused to worship the Babylonian idol, anyway" (cf. Dan. 3:17–18). My Masters students with religious backgrounds may be puzzled, and the two students who "got it" might be considered prodigies of Scripture by their peers; but seventy years ago, the entire British nation heard these words with appreciation. The three-word message galvanized citizens to launch across the channel every tug, every fishing boat, every craft that could float, and by means of "Operation Dynamo" not only the BEF was rescued but other allies as well, about a third of a million men. In 1940, the British people had a common heritage of the Scriptures, a shared tradition that was not simply cognitively understood but also effective and energizing.

To be a community means to have received and to retain a complex tradition that gives a common mind and a coherent life. To be a Christian means to have received and to retain, with gratitude, certain truths about God as revealed to us in the past; it means to have received life and to live in a certain way, following in the steps of the One who is the Christ. It also means to pass on what we have received to others, because there is and *so that* there is an intimate connection, a covenant, a *koinōnia* between brothers and sisters past, present, and future. In speaking of this phenomenon, Pelikan calls helpful attention to the surprising wisdom of Edmund Burke, who spoke about a "partnership not only between those who are living, but between those who are living, those who are dead, and those who are to be born."[6] If a partnership across the ages was seen as a necessary condition by Burke, that social philosopher and activist who put mere property at the base of human community, how much more should we, as Christians, lay claim to such a dynamic?

Yet there remains a dilemma. With various degrees of discomfort, most Christians of the twenty-first century acknowledge that there is a marked theological and even ethical dissonance among those who call upon Christ. Frequently we disagree regarding what actually *constitutes* the Christian partnership or family—what *is* the Church, and what is its make-up? More than that, we have dissonant views concerning our received and transmitted faith (what we believe) and trace in different contours the shape of the life that we share (how we should live). With such diverse formal, conceptual, and practical perspectives, how can Christians of different formations reason together about tradition? Now, it is true that a search for "the lowest common denominator" probably cannot provide an adequate basis for authentic and reliable unity. (Witness the difficulties now being experienced by the United Church of Canada, which began as a compromise between doctrinally diverse Methodist, Reformed, and Congregationalist communities. Or consider the merger of more alike, yet still diverse, Reformed churches that made up the Presbyterian Church [U.S.A.], whose continuing unity now seems precarious as various congregations and presbyteries are in serious disagreement.) However, a common denominator can provide us with a starting point for this difficult discussion, across Christian traditions, on tradition.

Virtually all Christians recognize a specific authority from their shared past—the Scriptures of the Old and New Testaments (though the boundaries of the older testament are variously marked by different Christian groups). Since Christians typically meet together to worship and live, rather than practicing individualistically, they also cleave to various traditions, or customs, around which they meet and agree—ways of stating what they believe, ways of praying, ways of worshiping together, ways of living. In some Christian groups, these

6. Ibid., 20.

traditions are clearly described and outwardly acknowledged; in such cases, tradition (often spelled with a capital *T*, Tradition) forms part of their faith and is spoken about as instrumental in the makeup of the Church. For others, certain practices and beliefs are simply followed, without a great deal of attention being given to how these customary ways have come about. They are like the spectacles by which a certain group of Christians sees the world or even reads the Bible: some groups pay attention to the spectacles, and others hardly notice that they are wearing them. So, then, a conversation and debate about tradition may begin well by giving due weight to the scriptural witness, but even this is not as straightforward as it may seem to some. At every turn, the Bible and tradition, or traditions, are intertwined.

Many evangelical Christians, for example, have a daily "quiet time" because that is how they were taught at home or what was recommended to them at the time of their conversion. This is, of course, an evangelical "tradition"—something expected of faithful evangelicals as the best and most fruitful practice, though it does not find its way into statements of faith or promises made at the time of inclusion in the community. At the same time, there are also historical traditions to which Christian groups or denominations deliberately look back in times of uncertainty. Such respect for family ways is found even among Christians whose worship community emphasizes the principle of *sola Scriptura* (the Bible alone), those who might be skeptical of extrabiblical tradition as a formal value. (It might be helpful to pause here, however, and notice, with the help of Pelikan, that this is, paradoxically, a "full-blown tradition" of "antitraditionalism,"[7] and that this antitraditional mind-set is in some cases unconscious and received rather than adopted with understanding.)

Despite the general principle of "Scripture alone," we see frequently in our era of denominational upset and confusion that more and more Protestant leaders are advocating a return to roots. And so in many quarters we notice a careful and deliberate quest to understand the beginnings of their own denomination, whether in the sixteenth, nineteenth, or even early twentieth century. When disagreeing about church polity, Presbyterian or Christian Reformed leaders will stress

7. Ibid., 11.

the "Reformed" way of organizing their church. When worried about a decreased fervency among the people, Methodists will stress the "piety" enjoined by the Wesley brothers. In response to violence and debate concerning current involvement in Middle Eastern conflict, North American Mennonites emphasize their pacifist tradition. When in conflict over doctrine, Anabaptist thinkers will remind those in their care that no Christian is bound by any particular creed or confession but should read the Bible for himself or herself (ironically, a *traditional* Baptist position).

In practice, of course, these lines of denominational or confessional thinking become tangled because we live cheek by jowl with each other, visit each other's worship communities, borrow each other's music, read each other's books, and are influenced by each other. I remember well an incident from over ten years ago, when my oldest daughter, then a young teen, was sitting in her first class at a French Roman Catholic school in Québec. One of the Sisters of Mercy who administered and taught at the school invited students to raise hands if they wanted the rite of *réconcilation* with the visiting priest—confession and absolution, she meant. My daughter, ever intrigued by something she hadn't experienced, raised her naive Anglican hand, only to hear a helpful hiss behind her back. The young lady behind her whispered: "*Tu n'es pas obligée!* You don't have to. You're not Catholic." To which my daughter, thinking quickly, responded: "It's okay. There's nothing in the Bible against confession! And I *am* catholic, just not Roman Catholic!" Her homeroom teacher was so amused that she related what had happened to me at the parent-teacher interview, saying that she had never heard a Protestant defend the practice of confession to a Catholic—and on the basis of the Bible! I decided not to argue with her that we were also "catholic" because we respected the whole Church, past and present, and were not sectarians. Nor did I tell her the story my daughter had related, of when she heard one of the girls complaining that she did not want to go to confession. The nun's only response had been: "Too bad. It's just something one does, my dear!" My daughter had not been impressed. Surely there was a better reason.

These little vignettes illustrate various attitudes toward a traditional practice. For some of the girls, the tradition of confession was an obligation, something that they did not question but performed because they were Catholic. But the Catholic girl who balked at the confessional is not alone: I have heard other contemporary Catholics express uncertainty concerning its necessity or helpfulness, as they gesture toward the many changes since Vatican II and comment on how difficult it is for a layperson to determine what persists in the Tradition by its nature and what can change. For my daughter, confession was something relatively unknown, a religious practice to be weighed by the Bible and that should, if valid, be defensible by giving reasons. Of course, the Sister may well have suspected that her reluctant Catholic student was simply being awkward and that she was well aware of why a Catholic goes to confession—rather like a mother who is insisting to her three-year-old that she must eat peas when the little nipper is asking, yet again, "Why-y-y, mommy?" And, like the mother of the three-year-old, the Sister perhaps hoped that the girls who met with the priest for prayer that day would discover the "why" in the experience.

Where Does Tradition Fit?

How *are* Scripture, tradition, reason, and experience related? This actually is a huge question among theologians today, who disagree with each other even within denominational boundaries. It has been customary to distinguish between typical Protestants, classical Anglicans, and Roman Catholics concerning how they weigh these things. This is the usual description: Protestants hold to *sola Scriptura,* the Scriptures alone as the rule of faith and practice; Anglicans believe in Scripture, while also honoring the place of tradition and reason in making hard decisions; and Roman Catholics have two authorities, Scripture and Tradition, with Tradition being expressed by the councils and by the pope.

This is, of course, far too simple a set of pictures. Among Protestants, for example, there has always been a debate as to whether the Bible has a restrictive or a "veto" function. That is, should we only do and believe what is explicitly directed in Scripture, or should we be free to do and believe things so long as they are not forbidden or denied in Scripture? Considering this argument, we may go back to the

famous disagreements between Luther and Carlstadt in the sixteenth
century and to Luther's poignant question, "Where is it forbidden?"
concerning the elevation of the bread in the Eucharist. Moreover, the
proliferation of confessions or doctrinal statements that were framed
in order to consolidate various Protestant positions has made it clear
that in practical terms *sola Scriptura* amounts to *prima Scriptura*
("Scripture in first place").

For example, even Harold O. J. Brown, who often has been characterized (caricatured?) as unbending in his particular Protestant views,
speaks about how tradition is a necessary part of the Christian life
(personal and corporate) but insists, as well, that tradition should be
treated with care. Scriptures ought not be opposed to tradition, he
suggests, but should be understood as the *norma normans*—the standard that brings everything else into line. Without tradition, however,
he says that worship, fellowship, community, and life would prove
difficult to maintain, though "salvation" may be established through
the Bible alone. In his understanding, tradition is the outward part of
the Christian life, akin to drinking vessels, clothing, and the matrix
in which we live.[8] Though some would find such a dualism (salvation
versus Church, inside versus outside) problematic,[9] Brown's words
serve to show that even in Protestant circles tradition is gaining more
respectability. There remain, of course, Protestant groups that are
more intransigent—or, we might say, more consistent—so that they
continue to resist the development of even confessional statements to
guide their group's interpretation of the faith. But even here the very
stance of *sola Scriptura* is guarded, paradoxically, as a treasure—a
tradition to safeguard the liberty of the Christian.

We find, then, a variety of approaches to the relationship between
Scripture and tradition in Protestant circles. This relationship is at
times carefully parsed (as with Brown or the newer movement that
has endorsed "A Call to an Ancient Evangelical Future"[10]) but at other
times simply intuited. When we move over to the Roman Catholic
communion, we find (as we might expect) that these matters have

8. Harold O. J. Brown, "Proclamation and Preservation," esp. 73 and 84.
9. Some of these are clarified in Melton, "A Response to Harold O. J. Brown."
10. This movement was initiated by Robert E. Webber and continues beyond his
death. Its website may be found at http://www.aefcall.org.

been more formally and judiciously considered. Indeed, Catholic theologians have spoken about the relationship between Tradition and Scripture in various and complex ways. (In speaking of Catholicism in its own terms, we must write Tradition with a capital *T*, since this is how that faith community distinguishes between Holy Tradition, which remains constant, and human or pragmatic traditions that are mutable.) In Catholic discussion, some seem to depict Tradition and Scripture as two parallel authorities; in other accounts, the Scripture is described as sufficient but requiring interpretation by means of Tradition; others portray Scripture as the written part of the apostolic Tradition. The influential and recently beatified Henry Newman described Tradition in terms of its "vigorous, energetic, persuasive, progressive"[11] qualities. Indeed, Newman considered the very development of Tradition to be that characteristic that demonstrates the Church to be "incorrigible,"[12] unshakable—an ecclesial unsinkable Molly Brown. In this light, he set forth the development of Catholic doctrine, including those dogmas that have disturbed Protestant sensibilities, in terms of a "sustained and steady march from implicit belief to formal statement,"[13] catalyzed in part out of reaction to various disturbances and heresies in the history of the Church.

In thinking about different Catholic articulations of the relationship between Scripture and Tradition, we are helped by the analysis of Richard Bauckham, who distinguishes three views: coincidence (Scripture and Tradition coincide); supplementation (Tradition supplements Scripture); and unfolding (Newman's view that Tradition is the unfolding of Scripture, and of Tradition itself at an earlier stage). These three views, even that of supplementation, are to be distinguished not only from the radical Protestant stance of *sola Scriptura* but also over against a more moderate Protestant view that admits tradition as an aid to explaining or applying Scripture, which Bauckham dubs the "ancillary view."[14]

Anglicans, with their "middle position," and their respect for the ancient creeds, have seemed to "split the difference" between the

11. Newman, *The Development of Christian Doctrine*, 438.
12. Ibid., 444.
13. Ibid., 439.
14. Bauckham, "Tradition in Relation to Scripture and Reason," 118.

Protestants and Catholics. They have also talked about the importance of the human reason in remaining faithful to Scripture and tradition (or Tradition, if we are listening to Anglo-Catholics). The great theologian Richard Hooker (1554–1600) is said to have invented the "three-legged stool" approach, and many claim this as the special Anglican way. By this, not a few Anglicans mean that Hooker established three authorities for Christians in the making of decisions—Scripture, Tradition, and Reason. This is misleading. Hooker was reacting to the Puritans of his day, who were refusing to allow certain practices in the church because they were not explicitly commanded in Scripture. Sing only Psalms, nothing else; don't have an order of bishops, priests, and deacons, because this isn't found clearly in Scripture; don't put candles on the altar. Again, Hooker was concerned for the anarchy that could set in once knee-jerk reaction replaced reason and the traditions of the whole Church were forgotten. Every Protestant might well become his or her own little pope—all the wisdom of past Christian ages could easily be forgotten!

This is the same quandary in which we see our friends the Jehovah's Witnesses, who say that the word "Trinity" isn't found in Scripture, so it is unbiblical. What Hooker taught was *not* that we have three *separate* authorities to which we can go to understand what to believe and how to act. He taught, rather, that Scripture was to be understood within the context of tradition—especially the creeds and councils of the undivided Church—and by the light of God-given, redeemed reason. Scripture was not to vie for place with tradition and reason as though these were three separate voices. Instead, reason and tradition were aids in understanding the Scriptures. And reason was to be used when the Church gathered together to worship, both in times of corporate prayer and during the hearing and interpretation of the Word of God. Of course, this is the very procedure recommended by St. Paul in 1 Corinthians 14: "If you bless with the spirit, how can any one in the position of an outsider say the 'Amen' to your thanksgiving when he does not know what you are saying?" (14:16); "Let two or three prophets speak, and let the others weigh what is said" (14:29).

So Anglicans, though seeking a mediating way, also quarrel. Do Scripture, tradition, and reason stand on level ground like a "three-legged stool," or is the better image that of a tricycle, with Scripture as the main wheel and reason and tradition following behind to keep the reading on track? (I am, myself, allergic to three-legged stools, ever since I tipped off one of these onto a concrete landing while painting a window, with the result of a concussion and a night spent in the hospital!) Nor are such questions merely academic. The model that one uses matters. Some Anglicans use the criterion "what is reasonable" to interrogate those parts of the Scriptures that are uncomfortable to our generation, whereas others will only allow tradition to perform as a guide where Scripture is silent. I suppose that historically Anglicans have adopted what could be called a *prima Scriptura* position. However, while working toward Church unity in mission situations, they have commended other Christian elements besides the Bible: Christians should respect not only Scripture but also the creeds, the sacraments (with words and elements used by Jesus), and the historic episcopate.[15]

As we move into more recent denominational discussion, we come face-to-face with an influential position from Methodism (specifically, from a twentieth-century theologian named Albert C. Outler). Many contemporary theologians, not simply Methodists, have adopted his idea of the (so-called) "Wesleyan Quadrilateral": the quartet of Scripture, tradition, reason, and experience. Thinking that they are following Outler's lead, and indeed also wrongly appealing to the eighteenth-century theologian and evangelist John Wesley (who would not have put these four things on an equal footing), they see these as equally valid foundations for personal and Church decision making. Wesley was certainly concerned in his day that Christians be more than simply formally "orthodox" in their beliefs. He yearned for every Christian by name to have a living experience of the Lord. As Outler rightly describes Wesley's practical theology, he was an "evangelical catholic" who displayed "a theological fusion of faith and works, Scripture and tradition, revelation and reason, God's sovereignty and human freedom" in which "the initiative is with God, the response is with man."[16] In indicating what Methodists were to be taught, Wesley appealed first to Scripture but then also to tradition as a "competent, complementary witness" to the meaning of Scripture. He went on

---

15. I refer to the Chicago-Lambeth (1886) Quadrilateral, proposed both as a guide to Christian unity and as a minimal standard for Anglican identity.
16. Outler, *John Wesley*, iv.

to admit that Scripture and tradition required "the good offices . . . of critical reason," and also to emphasize that "vital Christian experience . . . of the assurance of one's sins forgiven . . . clinched the matter."[17] Outler goes on to describe Wesley's approach as a "complex method, with its fourfold reference." Moreover, he notes that the method "preserves the primacy of Scripture, . . . profits from the wisdom of tradition, accepts the disciplines of critical reason," and places the "stress on the Christian experience of grace."[18]

Exaggerating Wesley's emphasis on experience, some quadrilateralists since Outler have argued that experience was the *main* thing for Wesley and that he actually placed it alongside Scripture, tradition, and reason as an equal authority or as a criterion for making decisions. Like a literal quadrilateral, all four sides are deemed important: Scripture, tradition, reason, and experience. Outler himself, who coined the phrase "Wesleyan Quadrilateral," later regretted it, since (in his own words) "it has been so widely misconstrued"[19] as an *empirical* means of *knowing* over against the way that Wesley talked about these four elements as instrumental in personalizing salvation. In this same reflective essay, written when he was nearing eighty in the mid-1980s, Outler lamented that there had even been, in the Methodist ranks, "a reduction of Christian authority to the dyad of 'Scripture' and 'experience.'"[20] One wonders what Outler would have thought of the far more radical tendency seen in some quarters today, when revisionist theologians make the fourth member of the Quadrilateral, experience, the trump card or the arbiter in debated moral and theological issues. After all, what a solitary individual experiences is likely to remain unintelligible, unless interpreted by means of rational processes and within the context of communal wisdom (that is, tradition).

Unfortunately, while recognizing the fallout today, when experience frequently is being made to bear a burden for which it is unsuited, Outler never seems to have clarified whether all of the four are meant to function as both *sources* and also *authorities* in theological thinking. There is no reason to debate the fact that each of us, and all of

17. Outler, "The Wesleyan Quadrilateral in John Wesley," see esp. 9.
18. Ibid., 10.
19. Ibid., 16.
20. Ibid., 17.

us as members of a faith community, have recourse to our experiences, to the operation of reasonable thinking and discourse, to past traditions (corporate experience?), and to Scripture, and that these may be roughly designated "sources" for theologizing or for making ethical or ecclesial decisions. However, it is another matter to assume that this makes experience and reason "authorities" in the same sense that the Church has recognized Scripture and, in many cases, Holy Tradition or even specific traditions. (In the following chapters, I will use the lower case "tradition" to refer to the concept in general and when speaking about Protestant discussions of tradition, while reserving the capitalized "Tradition" for what appears to be normative and binding Tradition in Catholic, Orthodox, or Anglo-Catholic contexts. I will also use "tradition" and "traditions" when referring to practices or ideas that may be ancient but are not clearly a part of Holy Tradition from the perspective of those communities that honor those things formally passed on as authoritative.)

However, Outler does not discern the difference in the way that experience and reason actually operate, as compared with Scripture and Tradition (or tradition). It might have been helpful had he noted that the first pair (experience and reason) are *tools* or *means* by which we hear, understand, organize, appropriate, and apply the corpus of Scripture and the deposit of Tradition found in creed, hymnody, liturgy, the meditations of the Church fathers, and the like. (We should, of course, recognize that in the Scriptures themselves, as in past tradition, we may see the exercise of reason and some appeals to experience, especially communal experience. But these are not presented as authorities in and of themselves; rather, they are means by which we recognize what is authoritative.) Scripture and Tradition, then, are gifts that the Church has received, though their precise contours have been and continue to be argued; reason and experience are general human actions or encounters *by which* we understand. Moreover, Outler does not give any clear indication as to how we should arbitrate between criteria when Scripture, tradition, reason, and (personal) experience seemingly collide. Instead, in his attempt to control the damage caused by the term "Wesleyan Quadrilateral," he waxes rhapsodic, taking refuge in attractive rhetoric concerning how we ought to be "immersed" in Scripture, "truly respectful" of the past, "honestly

open to . . . critical reason," and "eagerly alert to the fire and flame of
grace" (i.e., our personal experience). As Methodist scholar William
Abraham ruefully remarks, this kind of "superb rhetorical flourish"[21]
does not rescue the Quadrilateral from its inherent instability.

Despite Outler's caveat, the radical left continues to exploit the
Quadrilateral. Abraham suggests that this is because the Quadrilateral represents a "hasty shotgun wedding" between unequal entities,
"scripture and tradition on the one side and . . . reason and experience
. . . on the other."[22] The contemporary use of the Quadrilateral is far
removed from Wesley's practical theology and has become a method
"for dilettantes."[23] Outler's schema is now employed "creatively" by
those expressing their disagreement with other Christians who appeal
to Scripture, or to Scripture and Tradition, as authoritative—"but
what about reason and experience?" cry these progressive minds. The
most natural move has been to exaggerate this challenge and to assume that if, by our own modern experience, we are better informed
than a particular part of the ancient (and more naive) Scripture and
body of tradition, then experience should act as the main authority,
the trump card in the game of theology. How we begin and how we
proceed in making decisions in the Church does affect outcome. Many
of the contemporary "hot button" debates in the Church are fueled by
fundamental differences concerning what constitutes reliable authority.

Amidst all these positions, there are other possible ways of relating
Scripture to tradition, reason, and experience, as we can see in several
academic volumes that bring together Christians from different backgrounds[24] to debate these matters. On the ground, of course, members
of various Christian communities bring together these dynamics in
various ways too, often without thinking very deeply about what
they are doing. In a time when church bodies are not hermetically
sealed tight one against each other, and when there is a great deal
of "circulation of the saints"—Christians moving from church to

21. Abraham, "What's Right and What's Wrong with the Quadrilateral?" Profes-
sor Abraham provided me with a manuscript copy of this trenchant essay, which has
appeared also in *Canadian Methodist Historical Society Papers*.
22. Ibid.
23. Ibid.
24. See, for example, the essays in Bauckham and Drewery, *Scripture, Tradition
and Reason*.

church, denomination to denomination—we can never assume that any one Christian holds the views historically associated with his or her church. I have met Roman Catholics who have never heard the phrase "Wesleyan Quadrilateral," but who justify abortion on the basis of reason and experience. I have met self-proclaimed *sola Scriptura* Protestants who believe unswervingly in a whole series of doctrines that cannot be found in the Bible—for example, scenarios cooked up by sensationalists who give predictive details concerning the end of the world, despite Jesus' warnings that we can't know such things.

My Quest (Learning from History and Context)

The confusion in all this was brought forcibly to bear upon me as I made my own Christian pilgrimage during my teens and twenties. My own childhood formation was in the Salvation Army, a movement to which I owe a great deal. The Army has as its first doctrine, "We believe that the Scriptures of the Old and New Testament were given by God, and that they only constitute the divine rule of Christian faith and practice." As a child, I memorized twelve doctrines (each doctrine memorized being rewarded with a quarter!) along with the names of the books of the Bible. We were catechized in "Junior Soldiers' class" as children and in "Corps Cadets" as youth. (We were not taught to recite the Apostle's Creed, though it is printed in the back of the official *Handbook of Doctrine*, a move that positions the Army within the broader context of apostolic and catholic theology.)

What worried me, as I grew older, was that the Salvation Army persisted (and persists) in its tradition of not practicing the sacraments, despite the clear words of Jesus at the end of Matthew's Gospel (regarding baptism) and the teachings in the Gospels, Acts, and Paul (regarding the Lord's Supper). I heard entire sermons on the "Great Commission" (Jesus' closing instructions in Matthew's Gospel to his disciples to go into the world) that ignored the elephant in the room: here Jesus *commands* baptism as part of the apostolic mission. I was even more puzzled in Salvation Army meetings at the hearty singing of that gospel song "I've been redeemed by the blood of the Lamb," with its second verse: "And that's not all, there's more besides: I've been to the river and I've been baptized." "No you haven't!" I remember inwardly commenting. My young adulthood in the Salvation Army was a potent training ground not only for faithfulness, nor only for creating a disciplined desire to serve others, but also for the asking of hard questions about the nature of the Church and the place of tradition in Protestant churches. I became determined to take a look at the spectacles that were helping me to see and discovered that these were also blocking my vision. Eventually this quest led me to part ways with the Salvation Army (in terms of membership); yet I remain grateful for everything that I learned and for continued friendships there.

Like it or not, traditions and traditional ways of reading the Bible have brought Christians into strong disagreement and have been the catalyst for Church splits or impediments to reunion. At one point early in its history, the Salvation Army itself was asked to merge with the Anglican Communion and refused to do so because of the Army's commitment to the newly established tradition of female ministry and because of its stand regarding the sacraments. (To compensate, Anglicans copied the movement, and created the "Church Army.") Anglicans, keen on denominational reconciliation, proposed in the nineteenth century four ways of practicing Christianity called the "Lambeth Quadrilateral" (not to be confused with the "Wesleyan Quadrilateral"). These four principles were meant to be a kind of "lowest common denominator," something that could gather Christians of various backgrounds together. Even though they were very general, the four principles are not uniformly acceptable to all Christians. The problem? Tradition! One of the four principles is that the historic creeds truly describe the beliefs of Christians, but to recognize the creeds as authorities would be problematic for anyone who believes that he or she is committed only to the Bible and nothing else. Another of the principles the Lambeth Quadrilateral affirms is the importance of "historic episcopate" (the ongoing importance of bishops who have been consecrated by other bishops) as a basis for Church order. But there are Christians who do not consider the role of bishop (or priest or deacon) to be a biblical or necessary feature of the Church. So then, even the Anglicans, who consider their church as a kind of "bridge" between Protestants and Catholics, have not discovered how to help Christians agree about the place of tradition. Tradition and how we see things stand in the way.

Tradition also has played a big part in the actual separation of ways among Christians and Christian bodies. Wesley and his friend Whitefield, evangelists together in England, parted company over traditions of reading the Scriptures: Did the Bible promote the doctrine of "free will" (Wesley) or "election" (Whitefield)? Of course, one of the major reasons for the Reformation and the "protest" of that time was that the Reformers refused to accept particular traditions of the Church such as the selling of indulgences and masses for the dead. Their rejection actually went beyond a reaction to specific doctrines and practices to become a denial of the formal position that the medieval Catholic Church gave Tradition—as something alongside Scripture to be obeyed and honored. Yet the Reformers came to have their own ways of respecting the past and of passing this on. Both Calvinists and Roman Catholics continue to look back to the tradition that came from the ancient and blessed theologian Augustine of Hippo: Calvinists, however, discern in Augustine's writings the doctrine of election, whereas Roman Catholics stress other elements of his thought.

Going back even farther in time, we must remember the earliest major schism of the Church. The formal division between Eastern and Western Christianity threatened as early as the ninth century was total in the eleventh century and had several causes. A major reason for the break was, again, tradition and the question of who guards Holy Tradition. Could a universally accepted creed be changed after the fact by one section of the Church? And what authority does the Roman Patriarch, the pope, have in relation to the leaders of other esteemed historic churches? In all these debates, from the ninth through to the twentieth centuries, theologians, as well as "ordinary" Christians, have of course gone back to the Bible: but they read the Bible from particular perspectives, from within a tradition, acknowledged or assumed.

Beginning the Discussion

Since the turn of the millennium, we have heard more and more about the importance of tradition, ranging from doctrinally conservative individuals such as those responding to "A Call to an Ancient Evangelical Future," to the provocative work of David Brown concerning *Tradition and Imagination*. The Call to an Ancient Evangelical Future advocates that evangelicals "turn away from methods that separate theological reflection from the common traditions of the Church" and that they honor "the hermeneutical value of the Church's ecumenical creeds."[25] The challenge coming from David Brown's powerful work is more controversial. With William Abraham, I am pleased to see Brown's emphasis on the soteriological purpose of the Scriptures. However, I worry about the very broad strokes with which Brown paints tradition as God's "continuing revelation," so that he even commends us to move outside of Christianity (to the Qur'an, for example) in order to enrich our theological understanding and in order to reconfigure the problems of the twenty-first century.[26] Such proposals certainly indicate that tradition is getting better press today. But how do we, as Christians from different traditions, think carefully through these matters so that we may come to an understanding of traditions and Holy Tradition that goes beyond mere cherry-picking of those parts of the past that we happen to appreciate, or that is so broad an extension of the idea of tradition that we are set adrift in a sea of non-Christian historical practices and ideas?

There are many interrelated questions that will be exposed as Christians do their work together to come to terms with the value and place of tradition (and Tradition). Such an investigation will recognize that the word "tradition" is in some cases an abstract noun indicating beliefs, practices, and dispositions that have come to Christians from the past, while for the ancient Roman Catholic, Orthodox, and Anglo-Catholic communities, there are also established

25. "A Call to an Ancient Evangelical Future," available at http://www.aefcenter .org/read.html.
26. David Brown, *Tradition and Imagination*, 167. This very brief comment does not do justice to the depth and care of Brown's study, which deserves a reading even if readers find themselves unable to follow at some points. An in-depth analysis of Brown's argument in this book, including a consideration of his fundamental assumptions, has been penned by William J. Abraham, "Scripture, Tradition, and Revelation: An Appreciative Critique of David Brown." Prof. Abraham was kind enough to forward me a prepublication copy of this paper, presented at St. Andrews University, Scotland, in September 2010.

traditions that form part of normative Holy Tradition, spelled with a capital *T*.

The very fact that such explanations are necessary should tip us off to the difficulty of talking about such matters across ecclesial lines. Indeed, we should not assume that this discussion will move Christians immediately to a deeper unity, but that there will be, in the first place, a further complication of matters, indeed, perhaps an increased tension. (I think of the first time that I became aware of the Roman Catholic understanding of the Eucharist, complete with its teaching concerning who can appropriately receive at the altar. For years I had naively received the host while at the summer cottage, thinking that I was doing my part as a Salvationist to express unity with other Christians. When I came to understand that in the Catholic context the reception of the elements implied unity with the pope and acceptance of all Catholic dogma, and that in fact the pope forbade such reception, I had a twofold response: first, I was happy to understand more about the Catholic Church and its ecclesiology; second, I was now in tension when I worshiped there, the only place in that small community. My response was similar to a student of mine who was enamored with all things Eastern Orthodox until he stumbled upon their concrete ecclesiology, their claim to be the apostolic Church.)

Similarly, as we open the door to frank and careful thinking about Tradition, complicating questions emerge. I immediately think of three:

- Can we separate Scriptures from tradition? (Not everyone would agree that we can. For example, Pelikan reminds us that in the Christian faith, tradition both preceded the writing of Scriptures and proceeded after they had been written.[27])
- Is there a difference (and if so, what is it) between "traditions" and Holy Tradition? This typically has been answered in the affirmative by Catholics, Orthodox, and some Anglicans, but currently is being considered by those Protestants who are speaking

27. Pelikan, *The Vindication of Tradition*, 9. Pelikan further remarks that Luther thought that Tertullian (end of the second century) was the first Church father, so that there was a chronological gap between the writing of the New Testament and the ancient theologians: this is manifestly untrue. There is no gap between "gospel" and "tradition," at least chronologically.

with approval of "The Great Tradition." (See the conclusion of this book.) But how do we make the distinction?

- What is the relationship between the Church, Scripture, and Tradition? This question, of course, reminds us that wherever we start in speaking about our faith, we are dealing with a kind of seamless robe. The debates that began in the Reformation have doubled back in our day, so that for many people ecclesiology is *the* main issue facing Christians today. Tradition is a key element in our understanding of the nature of the body of Christ.

It is not my aim to solve all these problems but to make a start using a kind of "common denominator" approach, something shared by Christians: What does the Bible *really say* about tradition? Our major business will be to compare Scripture with Scripture, with all the help that we can get from others in the Christian community, past and present, who have read with care these texts that touch on the nature of tradition.

We want, as much as we can, to hear and discern *all* of what the Bible *really* says about tradition by looking at many of the places where it is spoken about, positively and negatively, as an action and as a gift. Where our denominational spectacles have served to block this sight, I hope we (and I!) will have the grace to take them off and try another pair. I do not here style myself as an expert, thinking that I can solve these problems on my own. Rather, I will deliberately enlist the help of Christians from various communities, past and present, as they read the Bible, in an effort to read the Bible with the whole Church. In our investigation, we will begin first with parts of the Bible that use the Greek terms most frequently translated as "tradition" in our English Bibles, the words *paradosis* and *paradidōmi*, words that include the idea of "giving" or "gift." As we begin the first chapter with a study of this word group, be prepared for a surprise: Has something been "lost in translation"? Chapter 1 will consider a host of scriptural passages that use the *paradidōmi* and *paradosis* word group, but will also touch on other places where the idea of tradition is evoked, but by means of other words.

In chapter 2, we will consider tradition in the transmission of the Bible (especially the Old Testament) and the teaching of the rabbis,

and then zero in on Jesus' condemnation of dead and deadly traditions in the Bible. Can we use the critique of the Law (or the rabbinic
understanding of the Law) by Jesus and Paul as a straightforward
commentary upon tradition? In this chapter we will consider the oral
and written aspects of tradition, and try to discern what the New
Testament means by a "dead letter" (2 Cor. 3) and a deadly tradition.

Chapter 3 looks carefully at teaching, practice, and worship in the
New Testament and considers the apostolic deposit that forms its
basis. In this chapter the decisions of the Church in Acts will provide
a good model for the understanding of tradition, while the debates
presided over by St. Paul in the Corinthians correspondence will
show us the importance of tradition in his ministry. The dynamics
that we see in chapter 3 will be amplified by the particular topic of
chapter 4, originally delivered as a sermon at Acadia University, in
which we will discuss God's "blessed delivery" to the Church. Attention to God's unusual means of delivery or transmission helps
us to see the many nuances and lively quality of tradition and how
it involves all members of the Church, not simply those in formal
leadership positions.

Chapter 5 discloses how the Bible considers tradition to be God's
personal gift to the Church, intimately connected with the giving of
the Holy Spirit. Chapter 6 probes, by means of the Scripture itself,
into the difference between Holy Tradition and human traditions, how
we can discern the difference, and what our stance might be toward
those "little traditions" that are not part of the immutable life of the
Church but that also are not noxious to Christians.

Finally, in our conclusion, we will touch upon what contemporary
Christian thinkers are calling "the Great Tradition": those continuing elements of the faith to which all Christians lay claim, including
not only a body of belief but also ancient writings, morals, worship,
and approach to life in general. We will revisit some of the early
Church fathers and trace the method by which they approached the
Scriptures—a method of reading the Old Testament that is in itself
part of Tradition, developing before, within, and beyond the writing of the New Testament. Our concern in all this is to discover the
stance of the biblical writings toward traditions and Tradition, and
to see how the approaches of the biblical writers set a good course at

the establishment of Christ's Church—a course in which we should continue because we share in their life.

In this study, I speak as one who was nurtured in the Protestant tradition and who has moved into a catholic and historic understanding of the Church, coming by way of Anglicanism into the Eastern Orthodox Church. While engaging in this process, I have discovered that confusion about the role of tradition is found in many places among Christians, even among those communities that value it. And, as we have noted, we are seeing in our day renewed interest in tradition and, among Christians, a keen desire to understand what some are calling the Great Tradition. This is going on in places where we might not expect it—let us say, in "untraditional" places. A half a block from my house, there is an evangelical church that sports a signboard with changing words. Once it declared that "A Sunday with God is better than Dairy Queen!" Most recently, it has enticed readers in this way: "We are untraditional; Check us out!" Many Christians would now smile with me in seeing this kind of advertisement, for that tradition of antitraditionalism is being questioned, as is the idea of the Church as a smorgasbord intended to meet different tastes. It is my prayer that all of us who look to Jesus will come to see our faith as a continuous and growing thing, something bound up with a common life, belief, and practice, something intertwined with the Scriptures, something that connects all of us together. With the apostle I pray that, with the eyes of our heart enlightened, we may know what is the hope to which he has called us, what are the riches of his glorious inheritance among the saints, and what is the immeasurable grandeur of his power for us who believe, according to the working of his mighty energy (cf. Eph. 1:18–19).

– 1 –

LOST IN TRANSLATION?

Despite it being uncomfortable to live in Québec as an English speaker at a time of social unrest, I am grateful for all that I learned while sojourning there during my early married years. Into a generational tradition that was wholly British (including England, Scotland, and northern Ireland), our family incorporated new ways of acting and celebrating: today my grandchildren consistently call me "grand-maman" because their mothers, born and raised in Québec and educated in French Catholic schools, want them to retain this adopted heritage. On birthdays we frequently sing *three* celebratory songs: "Happy birthday to you!," "God grant you many years" (from our Orthodox context), and *Ma Chère* whoever-it-is, *c'est à ton tour de te laisser parler d'amour . . .*" (I have never figured out quite *why* the Québecois think that the person who is having a birthday ought to have his or her "turn to speak about love," but it is an intriguing sentiment and represents the romantic French culture to a T). I have considered introducing my grandkids to the little ditty "Dropping, dropping, dropping, dropping, hear those pennies fall . . ." (the song I sang as a child while dropping birthday money into the Salvation Army lighthouse bank during Sunday school), but I suppose that four birthday songs might be stretching it!

Along with our expanded cultural repertoire, I also picked up (while teaching Bible in French, with great fear and trembling, to francophone university students) some riches that have helped me explain biblical studies to English-speaking students as well. One of these is to view the Bible as a *collection* of holy writings, full of different genres: the Greek term, *ta biblia*, the books, is very nicely illuminated by its cognate French word for library, *bibliothèque*. Another gem that I picked up was that it is notoriously difficult to draw the line between translating and interpreting, as the French verb for "to translate," *interpréter*, suggests!

This very ambiguity indeed can be seen in the Scriptures. In the biblical book of Nehemiah, when those exiles who had returned to Judah from Babylon and Egypt reassembled, the scribe Ezra read from the Torah, with his helpers "explaining the sense" to the people (Neh. 8:8 EH). Were they actually translating from the Hebrew because it had become a dead language to some second- and third-generation exiles, or were they interpreting and applying the Torah conceptually for the new context? And where is the line between these two services, translation and interpretation? This question is key, I think, to understanding what has happened in the English-speaking Christian world concerning our view of tradition.

As we noted toward the end of the introduction to this book, there are two terms in the Greek New Testament most commonly translated by the English word "tradition"—the noun *paradosis* ("tradition") and the verb *paradidōmi* ("to pass on," or, we might say, "to tradition"). So then, the related terms are compounds, coming from the Greek words *didōmi* or *dosis* ("I give," "gift") plus the preposition *para* (which has various meanings, including "alongside," "from the side," or "in proximity with"). The theologically astute might think of the title given to the Holy Spirit, the "Paraclete" ("the One called alongside"); the general public can think of "parachute"—that object which we dearly desire to have alongside us when we are jumping any distance! When we put all this together, we discern that the idea of tradition includes an act of giving (*didōmi*) over (*para*), a gift that is given over (*paradosis*), and an implied reception of that gift.[1]

---

1. The words can, in other contexts, refer also to surrender or betrayal, since the literal meaning is that of passing or giving over, or something passed or given over. So one could *give over* a criminal or one's own besieged city. But in the classical Greek

(There is a Greek verb that is typically associated with this reception, *paralambanō*, that we shall discuss later.)

In this chapter we will observe how the noun *paradosis* and verb *paradidōmi* are used in the New Testament and how these words have been translated in our complex tradition of English Bibles. Then we will engage in a general discussion of how some writers of the books of the Bible handled traditional material themselves, a topic that will be considered in more detail in chapter 2. Finally, we will touch on the many things in all their variety and splendor (some of them surprising) that are declared by the biblical writers to have been passed on to us as traditions. These, of course, we will see up close and personal throughout the rest of this book. These are "what we have received," gifts that we may receive personally and corporately, with thanksgiving. Among these gifts is even the Christian principle of "translation" and "interpretation," which is the focus of this chapter. Nor ought we to take this principle of translation for granted, since other faiths (e.g., Islam) do not think that their holy books can be fully or accurately translated. Though I will be making my argument by recourse to the original New Testament language, I do not want in any way to suggest that Christians without this expertise are intrinsically deprived of understanding or that "experts" in the original language are indispensable, like academic "priests" who have "the real stuff." God the Holy Spirit has his ways of communicating to us and does not *need* the ministrations of any experts, including those with skills in language. But, since we are in the body of Christ together, I pray that he will allow us to help each other where culture and language have conspired to obscure the truth, at least for a space of time and in a particular social context.

Let's begin with what the traditional and popular English translations make of these words *paradosis* (or plural *paradoseis*) and *paradidōmi*. Consider first Paul's often-forgotten words to the Corinthians: "I commend you because you remember me in everything, and keep the *paradoseis* just as I *paradidō*-ed them to you" (1 Cor. 11:2 EH). Now, compare this semi-English version (reminds me of Google

---

period, as well as in the New Testament era and the one that followed, the idea of tradition was one of the most common denotations of these compound words.

translate!), in which I have not even tried to transfer the *paradosis/ didōmi* words into English, with the translations of the Authorized Version and two other more recent versions:

- Now I praise you, brethren, that ye remember me in all things, and keep the *ordinances*, as *I delivered them to you.* (KJV)
- I praise you for remembering me in everything and for holding to the *teachings*, just as *I passed them on* to you. (NIV, 1973)
- I am so glad, dear friends, that you always keep me in your thoughts and you are following the *Christian teaching I passed on* to you. (NLT)

Well, I suppose it is understandable that English stylists wouldn't make up an English verb where there is none, and I don't expect the verb "to *paradidō*" or even "to tradition" to catch on, though stranger things have happened. (Academics now "bracket" ideas, and everybody and everything "impacts" everybody else. The newest Webster Dictionary classes "impact" as a transitive verb instead of simply a noun, to which use it was restricted when I was a student.) So, then, we can accept "delivered" and "passed on" as reasonable English paraphrases for a nonexistent verb. But where is the plural noun *paradoseis* in the KJV, the NIV, and the NLT? Nowhere! Instead, we hear the words "ordinances," "teachings," and "Christian teaching"—never "traditions," the most natural translation. Why do we think that might be? Did the Protestants of Elizabethan England not use the word "tradition"? Why, of course they did, but not with positive overtones! And the original[2] NIV and NLT simply followed the lead of the KJV (an interpretive *tradition*), since these versions were expected to flourish in the communities that traditionally had used the Authorized Version.

We see a similar situation when we analyze the translation of a more practical passage written by the apostle Paul. To the Thessalonians, some of whom thought that Jesus was returning imminently, he gave

---

2. The NIV has had several revisions since its first appearance. The verses in question recently have been altered (2011 version) so as not to obscure the references to "tradition." This is in itself a good indication that evangelicals no longer react with disapproval to the idea and that there is more attention being paid to the importance of historical roots and church tradition(s) in these circles.

this instruction about the importance of continuing on in their daily duties in life. We render it in the 1973 NIV translation:

> In the name of the Lord Jesus Christ, we command you, brothers, to keep away from every brother who is idle and does not live according to the *teaching* you received from us. (2 Thess. 3:6)

First, let's pause to notice that here in the original Greek we encounter the flip side of the active verb "to tradition" (*paradidōmi*); we learn from Paul that the congregation has *received* (*paralambanō*) Christian tradition. However, as in our first example, the NIV translators do not give a single nod to the word *paradosis*, this time used in the singular by Paul: "the tradition." Instead, they have Paul refer to "the teaching" received by the Corinthians—but Greek has a perfectly good word for teaching, and it is not *paradosis*. (It may be that the original conveyors of the NIV were instructed by the Tyndale Bible and the Treacle, or Bishop's Bible, which also avoid "tradicion" at this point and opt for the more narrow term "institucion.") We must give the translators of the older KJV credit in this case, for they do use the word "tradition" here. However, that KJV translation has traditionally (!) been accompanied in Protestant circles by explanations such as the following, found in Adam Clarke's famous commentary:

> This [word *paradosis*] evidently refers to the orders contained in the first epistle; and that first epistle was the tradition which they had received from him. It was, therefore, no unwritten word, no uncertain saying, handed about from one to another; but a part of the revelation which God had given, and which they found in the body of his epistle. These are the only traditions which the Church of God is called to regard.[3]

"Tradition," according to Clarke's accounting, cannot possibly be a reference to something oral, because that is a shaky foundation; rather, Paul must be referring back to another part of the *written* word, such as his first letter. The problem with this commentary is, of course,

---

3. Adam Clarke's *Commentary on the Bible* was originally published in eight volumes from 1810 to 1826 and became so popular that it is readily available in many forms, including its attachment to various computer packages for the study of the Bible today. The passage in question may be seen online at http://www.studylight.org /com/acc/view.cgi?book=2th&chapter=003. Accessed January 2012.

that it ignores what we have already seen in 1 Corinthians—that Paul indeed enjoins his followers to pay attention to oral instruction and not simply to his written letters. (Moreover, it may well be a mistake to distinguish tradition as oral over against Scriptures as written, as we shall see in the next chapter.) But translators subsequent to the KJV typically have followed the cue of such persistent explanations, expunging the offending word and replacing it with something like "teaching," such as the NIV translation we have just read. Or, consider this rendering:

> And now, dear brothers and sisters, we give you this command with the authority of our Lord Jesus Christ: Stay away from any Christian who lives in idleness and doesn't follow the *tradition of hard work* we gave you. (NLT, 2004)[4]

Here we may discern another subtle way of curtailing the importance of what Paul is saying. The word "tradition" is used, but it is qualified. As a result, the wording implies that the apostle is simply referring to a specific tradition concerning hard work, something to which any reasonable person would assent, and a practice that Paul indeed *did* model for the Thessalonians (1 Thess. 2:9).

Well, indeed, in context Paul is speaking specifically about the importance of work. He is concerned for the Thessalonians who had heard alarming tales about the end of all things, rumors that induced some to cease their normal round of activity. But the translator has clearly moved from translation (which should simply speak of "the tradition" that Paul had passed on) to interpretation by supplying *for* Paul the phrase "of hard work." What if Paul's example of modeling hard work were part of a larger body of tradition concerning how to live as a Christian, a tradition that he had received from Christians such as Ananias? Remember how this reluctant Jewish Christian nurtured the convert Saul/Paul, and that he, by the Holy Spirit, had informed Saul/Paul that he would have hard missionary work as a chosen vessel of God and much to suffer because of the name of Jesus (Acts 9:15–16). The limitation of this new translation does not

---

4. Like the NIV, the most recent NLT (2007) does not obscure the most obvious meaning of the text, since it drops the qualifying clause. Here too it seems that the antitraditional tradition that has made its impact upon translation is fading.

leave open this possibility that Paul is referring to something larger, just as the use of the word "teaching" in the NIV also obscured the positive value of "tradition" articulated by Paul in his original words. No, these translations are taking liberties, following along the bias of the fabric woven in the turmoil of the English Reformation: they alter, explain away, or narrow the meaning of the word "tradition" in accordance with preconceptions about what St. Paul must have meant. In contrast, the RSV (which certainly has its own bias) correctly delivers Paul's meaning when it translates our verse in this way: "Now we command you . . . in the name of our Lord Jesus Christ, that you keep away from any brother who is living in idleness and not in accord with *the tradition* that you received from us."

All this is not to say that the traditional English translations and those following them always avoid the word "tradition." No indeed! We find the word in spades in passages such as Colossians 2:8 or Mark 7:3–9, passages that are well known in churches associated with the Reformed tradition. So, for example, the NIV does not avoid the term when the Colossians are instructed: "See to it that no one takes you captive through hollow and deceptive philosophy, which depends on human tradition and the elemental spiritual forces of this world rather than on Christ" (Col. 2:8). In fact, this version, by dropping the definite article "the," which is in the Greek, and by turning the noun "human beings" into the adjective "human," paints the idea of "human tradition" in a broad sweep, as a general (and negative) phenomenon. In translating more literally, we should say "according to *the* tradition of human beings" rather than "which depends on human tradition." By referring generally to "human tradition" in a negative context, the translation predisposes readers to assume that all tradition is hollow, deceptive, and enslaving. Indeed, one either depends on Christ or on such pagan tradition, obeying *either* God or humans. We are sometimes called upon to make these choices, but other times God *uses* human beings to whom we should listen.

Again, when in Mark 7:3–9 we behold Jesus in controversy with the Pharisees, neither the KJV nor contemporary versions show the slightest delicacy in using the word "traditions" to criticize his opponents. After all, Pharisees are characterized among the faithful as not only sub-Christian but also as resisting Jesus *because* they were ritualistic:

For the Pharisees, and all the Jews, except they wash their hands oft, eat not, holding *the tradition of the elders*. And when they come from the market, except they wash, they eat not. And many other things there be, which they have received to hold, *as* the washing of cups, and pots, brasen vessels, and of tables. Then the Pharisees and scribes asked him, Why walk not thy disciples according to *the tradition of the elders*, but eat bread with unwashen hands? He answered and said unto them, Well hath Esaias prophesied of you hypocrites, as it is written, This people honoureth me with *their* lips, but their heart is far from me. Howbeit in vain do they worship me, teaching *for* doctrines the commandments of men. For laying aside the commandment of God, ye hold *the tradition of men*, *as* the washing of pots and cups: and many other such like things ye do. And he said unto them, Full well ye reject the commandment of God, that ye may keep *your own tradition*. (KJV, emphasis added)

Then there is the rendering of the NIV:

(The Pharisees and all the Jews do not eat unless they give their hands a ceremonial washing, holding to *the tradition of the elders*. When they come from the marketplace they do not eat unless they wash. And they observe many other traditions, such as the washing of cups, pitchers and kettles.) So the Pharisees and teachers of the law asked Jesus, "Why don't your disciples live according to *the tradition of the elders* instead of eating their food with defiled hands?" He replied, "Isaiah was right when he prophesied about you hypocrites; as it is written: 'These people honor me with their lips, but their hearts are far from me. They worship me in vain; their teachings are merely human rules.' You have let go of the commands of God and are holding on to *human traditions*." And he continued, "You have a fine way of setting aside the commands of God in order to observe *your own traditions*!" (NIV, emphasis added)

So, then, both the KJV and the NIV render the *paradosis/paradidōmi* group literally in this case. I am not certain why the NIV translates the singular Greek noun *paradosis* as plural in the last two verses ("human *traditions*"; "your own *traditions*"), unless it is on the assumption that these are arbitrary regulations and not part of a coherent body of teaching. But the NLT, which also persists in using the plural, is even more transparent. Listen for the dismissive phrases "ancient traditions" and "age-old customs," coupled with the plural "your own traditions." It interprets in this manner:

> (The Jews, especially the Pharisees, do not eat until they have poured water over their cupped hands, as required by *their ancient traditions*. Similarly, they eat nothing bought from the market unless they have immersed their hands in water. This is but one of many traditions they have clung to—such as their ceremony of washing cups, pitchers, and kettles.) So the Pharisees and teachers of religious law asked him, "Why don't your disciples follow our *age-old customs*? For they eat without first performing the hand-washing ceremony." Jesus replied, "You hypocrites! Isaiah was prophesying about you when he said, 'These people honor me with their lips, but their hearts are far away. Their worship is a farce, for they replace God's commands with their own *man-made teachings.*' For you ignore God's specific laws and substitute *your own traditions.*" Then he said, "You reject God's laws in order to hold on to *your own traditions.*" (NLT, 2004, emphasis added)

How interesting! The "elders" and the formal phrase "tradition of the elders" disappear entirely in this version. Instead it is insinuated that traditions are, by nature, "ancient," "age-old," or old-fashioned, and only according to "ceremony."

In all these comparisons, we have made a startling discovery. Several popular Protestant translations use the idea of "tradition" solely or mostly in conjunction with the Pharisees or in a negative context of pagan learning. If the word "tradition" is allowed to stand, its meaning is narrowed by an explanatory phrase or controlled by the commentators who are worried about how readers will assess the role of tradition. The inference most readers and students of these translations naturally make is that tradition is the purview of non-Christians, such as the Pharisees who centered upon Torah and oral tradition instead of Jesus, or of the confused pagans whose human traditions were arbitrary and mutually contradictory. (To be fair, I should point out that when the Catholic translation, the New Jerusalem Bible, translates the critical phrase in Col. 2:8 about hollow philosophy and traditions of people, it seemingly avoids the word "tradition"[paraphrasing this as what "human beings hand on"]—perhaps there is a reverse prejudice here!)

My point in all this is to indicate that often, when the original Greek noun or verb is used with a positive meaning, English translators employ paraphrastic words or phrases: not "tradition," but deposit of faith, teaching, doctrine, and so on. From the get-go, then, we have two problems. The first is the genuine difficulty of rendering these passages in English, since there is no English verb "to pass on as tradition" that is readily recognizable as there is in the Greek. (To put the word "tradition" into a phrase like this is unwieldy, and I understand the reluctance of translators to do so. However, if we had, as a Church community, a robust understanding of the value of tradition to the apostles, we would hear such words as "deliver" and "pass on" and immediately understand that the Scriptures were alluding to valuable and life-giving tradition.) The second difficulty is the real one. It is a matter of predisposition, a Protestant "tradition" of talking about tradition. We assume, because of the problems of the medieval Church, that tradition in itself is a bad thing, a declension from the truth of the gospel, when that is an overreaction that is not borne out by Scripture itself. There remains, then, the difficulty of rendering the verb. (Can I persuade us to adopt the verb "to tradition"?) Coupled with this, there is an ingrained prejudice against "tradition" by some Christian "traditions." Because of our language and because of the way that translators influence us, English readers are frequently shaped to adopt a negative view of tradition, and this needs to be rethought.

"To Tradition"

Generally, I do not think highly of the creation of new words (except by those with the genius of Lewis Carroll), especially making verbs from nouns. However, sometimes it is helpful. It is awkward that English does not have a single verb meaning "to deliver as a tradition." Call again to mind that the Greek has a noun, *paradosis*, and a related verb, *paradidōmi* (plus less-used compounds like *epididōmi* also connected with the verb "I give"), as well as a complementary verb *paralambanō*, which refers to receiving tradition and also uses the preposition *para*. The New Testament is replete with these verbs, and often they do not receive a translation that will call attention to them as a cluster of words that connote the idea of tradition. (This is a similar situation to the problem English speakers have in reading Paul accurately on "justification," "to justify," and "justice"—we don't easily recognize from our translations that these words are in the same word group and indeed sometimes identical with words that we translate as "righteous" and "righteousness." But that is another story.) Returning to our discussion of tradition in the Bible, it is helpful to remember that whenever we encounter in the New Testament the word "deliver" or the phrase "pass on" on the one hand, or the word "receive" or the phrase "what you have received" on the other, our ears should prick up. These are words linguistically and technically, and not simply conceptually, connected with the idea of tradition.

What *does* the Bible have to say about tradition? First, it would be useful to take note of the manner in which the biblical writers themselves "traditioned," or handled, traditional material. In most introductory courses on both the Old and New Testaments, in both colleges and seminaries, professors take a great deal of time talking about "form criticism," "source criticism," and "redaction criticism." Some of these disciplines rely on conjecture and speculation, of course.[5] Despite the disparate results and the guesswork involved in these scholarly interventions, there is still an uncontestable foundation provided in the Bible itself for questions about oral forms, written sources, and the redaction of these materials. That is, students of the Scriptures encounter in the books that they read a very interesting double phenomenon. First of all, in many ways, the books of the Bible read as consecutive narratives, and indeed, following the cue of some of the Psalms and letters of St. Paul, we can aptly describe the entire canon as an overarching metanarrative of God's dealings with humanity and with Israel. The creation story in Genesis is followed by the fall, then by the story of the patriarchs, and so on. Or the double volume of Luke-Acts begins with the birth and infancy narratives of Jesus, offers a genealogy, and proceeds through the beginning of Jesus' ministry in Nazareth, to his mission in Galilee and Jerusalem, to his death, resurrection, and ascension, and then on to the continuing mission of the apostles.

5. For a very good analysis of these methods, and how they are conceptually related, I recommend Barton, *Reading the Old Testament*.

Or consider the shape of the canon as a whole. Genesis, the story of primeval beginnings, provides the first of a set of bookends, with the other one seen in the book of Revelation, which envisions the anticipated new heaven and new earth. In between, in our arrangement of books and following a rough chronology, we move from the patriarchs, to the judges, to the kings, to the exile, to the time after exile, to the writings and prophets that illumine this great story of Israel, to the coming of John the Baptist and the gospel story, to the letters and writings that illumine the story of Jesus. Some scholars who pore over the arrangement of the canon[6] have endeavored to show how the contrasting arrangements by the two communities who use the Old Testament writings, the Jewish and Christian communities, show the different way that these groups have understood this history. Certainly the New Testament writings implicitly offer a Christian method of interpreting the Hebrew Scriptures, an essential element of what the ancient Church called the *regula fidei*, the rule of faith. Those writings, they claim, pointed forward to Jesus.[7]

However, cutting across and through and in the midst of this continuity is found a second startling phenomenon of irregularity or choppiness. This occurs not because the ancient writers were incapable of smoothing out rough edges, of editing well—indeed, they do this on a regular basis.[8] Rather, it seems clear that in many cases they did not desire wholly to obscure the past and left traditions side by side even when this was not felicitous artistically. As an analogy, remember that Roman Catholics (also Anglicans and Russian Orthodox) continue to sing the ancient Greek chant *Kyrie Eleison* whether or not they are celebrating in Latin, English, or Russian. In fact, I have been to contemporary mainline

6. See, among others, the following volumes: Roger Beckwith, *The Old Testament Canon of the New Testament Church* (Grand Rapids: Eerdmans, 1986), 181–234; F. F. Bruce, *The Canon of Scripture* (Downers Grove, IL: IVP, 1988); and various articles in Lee M. MacDonald and James A. Sanders, eds., *The Canon Debate* (Peabody, MA: Hendrickson, 2002).

7. Fr. John Behr, in his *The Way of Nicea*, speaks on pp. 30–44 about the "rule of faith" and on p. 37 about the significance of the apostolic "mode of interpretation" of Old Testament Scripture as a primary component of the ancient "rule of faith."

8. On the paradoxical method of Old Testament redaction critics and how redaction criticism can, unwittingly, remove the foundation on which it stands (form and source criticism), see the amusing and incisive analysis of Barton, *Reading the Old Testament*, 57.

Protestant churches that have adapted this ancient chant for Lent without translating it for twenty-first-century ears. Such communities care enough about the roots of Christian liturgy not to obliterate a key part of it, even though the Greek does not match its new surroundings.

The same phenomenon is found in the Bible as a whole and in its smaller parts: traditional prayers, hymns, and stories are incorporated, sometimes without notice, into a larger corpus of more recent origin. Scholars, of course, argue about whether they have detected such seams and irregularities when they do minute analysis of the Bible. But most agree that there appear to be, for example, two original creation accounts, the first comprising God's creation of the seven days, ending at Genesis 2:4a, and the second focusing more upon Adam and Eve, continuing to the fall. "Redaction" critics of the Pentateuch (the first five books of the Bible) endeavor to show how the final writer of these books knit together traditions that came from various places, whether from the Northern Kingdom, or Judea, or from the priestly group, or wherever. But they have no independent evidence for these earlier traditions—they rely upon the choppiness of the text, the point where the text retells a story, variations or discrepancies in detail, and so on, to indicate where we may be dealing with disparate sources. The famous example would be the Noah story, where in one place Noah brings in the animals two by two, but in another he is told to bring in the kosher animals by sevens and only the ordinary animals by twos. As the text reads, the notice about the seven is not given as a refinement or a correction but just enters the text abruptly—thus, we are surprised at the discrepancy.

And it gets even more complex. For we have two different accounts, separate by title, of the Jewish kingdoms—one found in 1 Samuel through 2 Kings, the other in 1 and 2 Chronicles. These versions, not joined together but sequential in the Christian organization of the canon, present some real quandaries when we read them synoptically (in parallel) at the places where the stories overlap. Who *did* tempt David to engage in a proud census of his people (2 Sam. 24; 1 Chron. 21)? The LORD, as the Deuteronomist[9] would have it? Or Satan, as

9. The Deuteronomist is the name some scholars give to the theoretical writer of the first saga of Judah/Israel (usually traced from 1 Samuel through 2 Kings).

the Chronicler insists in more politically correct fashion—after all, would the righteous LORD tempt, then punish? Both the Jewish and Christian communities have kept both versions, unwilling to allow the correction of the Chronicler to override the first version. Perhaps we need both seemingly incompatible explanations—one that celebrates God's sovereignty, another that reminds us, with James, "God tempts no one"? Though puzzling, the two passages, when read together, help us work through the mystery of sin and evil in a nuanced and faithful manner.

Or what about the Gospels—there are three that can be put side by side, and a Fourth that is in some ways quite different from, and in other ways harmonious with, the Synoptics. Luke the evangelist even describes to us the hard work of researching and putting in order what had happened among the Christians and acknowledges that others had undertaken to write accounts. The differences between these versions, and of the three Synoptics over against the Fourth Gospel, are manifest, and indeed provide grist for scholarly mills of creative historical reconstruction. The first-time reader who is sensible to detail naturally asks: So then, did Jesus take the disciples up the mountain on the sixth day after Peter's confession or the eighth? And on what day was he crucified? Before or on Passover?

It is not as though ancient Christians were stupid or did not notice such problems. Certainly they could have cleaned things up, retaining only one Gospel, redacting bits of others, or even composing a Gospel harmony out of the evangelical raw material that would become authoritative. They did none of these things. Clearly they were keen to keep and respect all the apostolic witnesses, and for them that did not require a harmonization that would remove these problems. One early theologian, Marcion, tried to remove the contradictions he perceived between the ancient Old Testament and the Christian gospel—and we know what happened to him! (His efforts were not appreciated but condemned as heretical.) Another noteworthy from the past, Tatian, wrote a continuous narrative, a gospel harmony that eliminated the seams—but it was not this *Diatessaron* that was recognized as preserving the canon of truth or faith. Rather, the Christian community has, throughout the ages, been challenged by the four Gospels together, in all their many-colored and differing glories. In the same way, we continue to read as a community a personal letter to a slave owner (what an odd document for sacred Scriptures!), several letters that overlap in content (Colossians and Ephesians), Jude as well as 2 Peter (despite their strong similarities), and James alongside the collection of Paul's letters (even though that presented difficulties for the debate over faith and works).[10]

The principle of passing on things as received, even when this causes complications, is clearly traced. This is true not only when we compare biblical text with biblical text but also when we look at certain curious details in a single story. Traditions such as the weakness of St. Peter (both with Jesus and in the fight with St. Paul over table fellowship, cf. Galatians) and the bloody-mindedness of St. Paul have not been removed, but included, because they are part of the story.

Moreover, all this retention of embarrassing discrepancy and detail goes on while we have other evidence that the traditions were not woodenly passed on but were instead understood to have a living quality, inherently adaptable to different situations. Indeed, such a potent parable as the story of the prodigal and proper sons (with their extravagantly loving father) seems to have taken on a life of its own in the Church, beginning in Jesus' own day as a pointed comparison between the nonpracticing and renegade Jew over against the rigorous Pharisees, and becoming in Luke's Gospel a promise to the gentiles whom God loves in addition to his chosen people. Indeed, Jesus' parables and teachings are not found in identical wording from Gospel to Gospel, but in different modes. To have a homogeneous and bowdlerized[11] Bible, or even to drop the Old Testament, might have been more comfortable, and we have ample evidence that the early Christian community felt free in some cases to adapt its traditions for

10. Luther, of course, would have been happy to excise James, due to his stand for *sola fide* ("by faith alone"), but the antiquity of that letter's inclusion in the canon made such a move impractical.

11. Thomas Bowdler was the nineteenth-century English scholar who published an edition of Shakespearean plays and Gibbons's *Fall of the Roman Empire* that he deemed "suitable" for Victorian schoolboys by the removal of the racy bits. I doubt that his efforts (and those of his sister Harriet, who actually did the editing) would have been approved by their mother, Elizabeth Stuart Bowdler, who herself wrote a commentary on both the book of Revelation and the Song of Songs! See Humphrey, "Elizabeth Stuart Bowdler."

new situations. However, Jewish and Christian respect for the patriarchal, prophetic, and apostolic traditions seems to be part of their
hermeneutical DNA, so that the Bible and the faithful community
take on the form of a growing tree, not a succession of new subdivisions being built on a newly bulldozed neighborhood. The Bible's very
structure, how it "grew like Topsy," is a witness to a characteristic
Jewish and Christian care about tradition. In some aspects, the way
that the Scriptures have been compiled is more like the work of a
"preservation" society than the efforts of those who would "restore"
things to a pristine condition. Everywhere we look we see traditions,
and among these a current that makes sense as one single Tradition.

Identity through Rejecting Traditions

Reflection about how communities grow will also help us to see that
the forging, or rather the continuation, of an authentic tradition also
means the rejection of those things with which that stream is incompatible. We know this in natural life too—cells that do not die as
they ought to, in the balance of the body, cause cancer. Jesus' debates
with the Sadducees and Pharisees were recounted by the evangelists
not simply to show his excellence in critical analysis, his verve, or his
ability to triumph over enemies. The encounters were related in the
Gospels in order to instruct, to mark off the ways that Christians were
not to follow. As St. Paul puts it with regard to the stories of Israel's
failures, "These things are written to mark off a negative pattern, for
our admonition" (1 Cor. 10:11 EH). In the next chapter, we will see
that the problem with the Jewish groups of Jesus' day, whether the
Temple party of the Sadducees or the Torah party of the Pharisees,
was *not* that they were "traditional" and therefore closed to novel
teaching Jesus-style. It was that they had not properly traced the action of God in the past, that they were elevating or exaggerating good
things beyond their original purpose, and that they had blinders on
regarding God's mode of action among them both in the past and
in their own day. After all, Jesus constantly refers back to the Torah,
to the conventional sayings of the wisdom writings (including those
classed in the collection known as the Apocryphal/Deuterocanonical/

Readable books), or back to the *tradition* of the king-defying prophets in trying to correct these groups. About the time that Jesus came on the scene, there were multiple opposing ways of expressing one's Jewish faith (more than four parties that we can call "Judaisms"). With the advent of God the Son, sense was made of this multiplicity; with Jesus, there came a clarification, a fulfillment, and a completion of the biblical story to which these Judaisms laid claim, as the One called Word and Wisdom summed up God's plan for Israel (and humanity) in himself.

Of course, there are deadly traditions that can obscure or even block what God intends for us to hand down in the family. To note this is not an indictment of tradition per se. Rather, the difficulty occurs when too much emphasis is placed on any thing, even any penultimately good thing such as Torah or Temple or purity laws. When this happens, these things that are good in themselves obscure or stand in the way of God, preventing us from seeing the ultimate One who shows us who God is and what we are meant to be and do. Such mistakes are not made simply by pagans or by God's historic people, however. Remember the words of St. Paul that the Scriptures of the Old Testament were given as warnings for those who are in Christ, whether one's background is Jewish or gentile. We will consider this problem in the next chapter, as we turn to the rabbinic approach to tradition in comparison with Christian approaches and the Bible's critique of dead (or even deadly) traditions, whether oral or written.

Thanks be to God, however, who is our light! To help us in our darkness and in our proneness to wander, many traditions—good, helpful, and nurturing—have been bequeathed to us in Christ. These come in the form of words, documents, practices, and prayers, by means of the Spirit of the Lord. The archetypical inspiration to which the Church looks back is Pentecost, represented on the cover of this book through the icon "The Descent of the Spirit." In this icon we see the communion of the apostles depicted in their action of gathering (at a meal? in conference?), as well as in the rainbow-like arc that surrounds them. Down upon the Twelve streams the power of the Holy Spirit, coming as rays from the divine glory. Their authority is indicated by what they hold: either gospel-books (the four evangelists) or scrolls, symbolic of what they have received and will bestow on those who follow. The icon is transhistorical since it includes all four evangelists (not all of whom were strictly among the Twelve), St. Paul (at center right) who was joined to the number of apostles as one "untimely born," and the deacon Philip (bottom right). Moreover, the icon includes a promise of the Church to come, presented by the wooden door in their midst. In this Coptic version of the icon, the door remains closed, perhaps in deference to the scriptural detail that they were behind closed doors for fear of the authorities. In other classical depictions, however, within that door appears either a multitude of people coming from various directions or (a little later in the tradition) a solitary dark but kingly figure called "Cosmos" (the world). Cosmos represents the gentile nations, to whom the apostles will preach, and to whom Holy Tradition will be bequeathed. Henri Nouwen gives a helpful exposition:

> Pentecost is not the beautiful end of the salvation story, but the beginning of a mission to go out into the world, make disciples of all nations, baptize them in the name of the Father, the Son and the Holy Spirit, and teach them to observe all the commands that Jesus gave us (see Matthew 28:19–20). The same Spirit who binds the disciples of Jesus together into a vibrant community of faith, sends them into the world to liberate those who dwell in "darkness and the shadow of death" (Lk 1:79). . . . This Cosmos . . . represents all the peoples living in darkness to whom the light of the apostles' teaching has been brought.[12]

Perhaps it is particularly poignant for the purposes of this book that the door to Cosmos is closed. For me (idiosyncratically, no doubt) it recalls the tragedy that today Tradition is a closed or at least blocked door to many, even among those who name Christ. What happens when the door is opened and we allow the full deposit of the Spirit to shine upon our minds and hearts? The Scriptures, the written deposit, are our departure point.

When we gaze into the Scriptures, what do we find that has been delivered to us to keep and pass on, "traditioned" to us? Let's collect a few of these in closing, as a preview to the riches that we will encounter in the following discussion of tradition in the Bible:

12. Henri J. M. Nouwen, *Behold the Beauty of the Lord: Praying with Icons* (Notre Dame, IN: Ave Maria Press, 1987), 68–69.

- In Luke 1:2, we hear that the Gospel stories themselves are traditioned.

- In Luke 10:22, Jesus rejoices that *all good things* have been delivered to the Son by the Father, and then to the apostles by the Son.

- In Acts 15:30, 16:4, letters are delivered from the apostles to the church, which is to receive and honor these.

- In Romans 6:17, Paul says that we have been "traditioned" *to* a pattern of moral teaching; that is, our very lives have become part of the tradition to which this teaching also belongs.

- In 1 Corinthians 11:23, Paul uses the technical word for "reception" and "tradition" to speak about the communion service. (And we know that his version closely corresponds to that related in the Synoptics, especially Luke, concerning Jesus' last supper, which Paul did not himself attend, of course. He had received this from the Lord, by way of other Christians.)

- In 1 Corinthians 15:3, Paul uses the same language to give to the Corinthian church a formal list of those who had seen the risen Lord—and he includes himself in this tradition, though he is an irregular case.

- Jude 3 speaks of the faith once traditioned to the saints. By this he doesn't mean the attitude or sense of having faith but the body of what we believe, over against heresies.

- Most surprisingly, in John 19:30, we are told that the Lord Jesus, as he died, *traditioned* his Spirit. The Holy Spirit was bequeathed to the Church—later the apostle Paul will use the metaphor of an engagement token, a down payment. In the end, God's greatest tradition is himself, his presence in the Holy Spirit.

We finish by noticing a curiosity of the Greek verb "to tradition" or "to deliver"—it can also be used to hand someone over to death or to betray someone. And so Jesus himself, on the night that he was "handed over," actually was given into the hands of human beings. He was himself, if you like, God's greatest Tradition, for humans to keep or try to destroy—though no one could actually snuff out the One who is Light-from-Light. In this marvelous list, we see that tradition can include the actual body of doctrine or teaching, an interpreted story about Jesus, and practical teaching or instruction for living and Church order. Our bodies, our outside form, as well as our inside heart and belief are affected by what God has passed on to us.

I suspect that as we close this first chapter, some readers are demurring, "Well, fine, but all these things that have come by tradition are found written in the Bible now, aren't they? Everything that *they* had by tradition, *we* now have written down in the canon. *They* may have needed tradition before the Old Testament was canonized, before the New Testament documents were written, but *we* have the solid, concrete, written material, to which we should give our deepest attention." This is a common opinion among those who honor the Bible as their primary (or perhaps sole) authority. So we will, in the following pages, discuss what we lose if we confine our reception of Tradition to the written Word alone. What difference does it make to identify Christians not foundationally as "people of the Book," that designation that we often use for Christians, Muslims, and the Jewish community together? What if we stress, instead, the *personal*, and see ourselves as first and foremost "people of the Christ" ("Christ's ones," as they were called in Antioch)?

We have received the written Word and rejoice in it. But we have been joined to the Father because we have received the Incarnate Word, God the Son, and been drawn by means of the infused Wisdom, who is the Holy Spirit. Thanks be to God for his unspeakable gift!

━ 2 ━

DEADLY TRADITIONS

The Bible, the Rabbis, Jesus, and St. Paul

Give ear, O my people, to my teaching; incline your ears to the words of my mouth! I will open my mouth in a parable; I will utter dark sayings from of old, things that we have heard and known, that our fathers have told us. We will not hide them from their children, but tell to the coming generation the glorious deeds of the LORD, and his might, and the wonders which he has wrought. He established a testimony in Jacob, and appointed a law in Israel, which he commanded our fathers to teach to their children; that the next generation might know them, the children yet unborn, and arise and tell them to their children, so that they should set their hope in God, and not forget the works of God, but keep his commandments; and that they should not be like their fathers, a stubborn and rebellious generation, a generation whose heart was not steadfast, whose spirit was not faithful to God. The Ephraimites, armed with the bow, turned back on the day of battle. They did not keep God's covenant, but refused to walk according to his law. They forgot what he had done, and the miracles that he had shown them. (Ps. 78:1–11; 77:1–11 LXX)

With these words, Asaph composes a "maskil" (a traditional name for a Hebrew song, the precise meaning of which is now lost to us). The psalm, by its own accounting, is offered so that those who hear and recite its words will not forget the mighty deeds and the compassion of the LORD, as did the Northern Kingdom, the Ephraimites. In the first ten verses, we recover simply the principle that sacred tradition should be remembered and honored: to reclaim the tradition itself, we should have to recite the entire lengthy psalm, following its drama for seventy-two lengthy verses, from God's deliverance of the Hebrews in Egypt to their rebellion in the desert, from their short-lived repentance and happy entrance into the Promised Land to the perfidy of the priests and especially the Northern Kingdom (aka Ephraim), from the punishment and marginalization of the North to God's choice of Judah and Mount Zion as the holy heritage of the LORD. The psalm is celebratory of God's goodness and so is a spiritual act of thanksgiving. However, it is also political, preserving for us a human perspective—the viewpoint of the Southern Kingdom, Judah, which focused upon Jerusalem and trusted (perhaps uncritically and too literalistically) in the sure promises given to King David (cf. 2 Sam. 23:1–7; Ps. 132:11; 131:11 LXX). The arrangers of the Psalter, in their wisdom, follow this psalm of instructive confidence, with its implicit optimism regarding Judah, by the more sober Psalm 79 (78 LXX). In contrast to the preceding psalm, Psalm 79 begins by recognizing the defilement of the Temple and ends with a heartfelt prayer for God's returned favor, so that "the flock of [the LORD's] pasture" might again "give thanks . . . for ever, from generation to generation" (Ps. 79:13, 78:13 LXX).

The coexistence of Psalms 78–79 (77–78 LXX) provide for us another example of the complex ways in which tradition is handled in the Bible. As with the stories concerning David and the census, awkward traditions are retained (here, the mistaken belief that Judah would *not* be decimated like Israel) even while traditions are adapted in a lively manner to their new circumstances. In encouraging the people to praise and give thanks, and in encouraging the people to be self-critical and penitential, the Psalms together provide a rich and nuanced tradition that knits the community together and also interprets their unfolding history (as well as their present) to them.

In speaking about the role of traditions and why they are passed on in the Jewish context, James Kugel reminds us that "from a very early period, the texts that make up the Hebrew Bible were interpreted texts."[1] That is, the original stories and texts show their significance as they are *used*—reread, modified, interpreted, and, in these ways, passed on. An intriguing example of these dynamics makes its mark in the text of the Hebrew Bible, where we can discern the creative and communal use of Psalms 105, 96, and 106 (104, 95, 105 LXX), all of which include a cosmic direction proclaiming God as the King of the universe. These psalms are knit together in 1 Chronicles 16:7–43, the dramatic narrative in which David brings the ark into Jerusalem. In the context of Chronicles, the cosmic aspect is muted (for the incoming is a national event), and the Psalms' references to Jerusalem are generalized to speak about "God's holy place" (for the temple, in the sequence of the story, had not yet been built). Moreover, the setting of Chronicles shows us that, from the perspective of the Chronicler, the Psalms had taken their place in the traditional worship of the Jewish people: David, says the Chronicler, on the day that the ark came into Jerusalem, appointed these songs to be sung. But in the singing, these psalms were shaped by the understanding of later Judeans who knew of the split between North and South, who venerated the temple, and who had come, in their exile, to recognize the need of the nations for God's blessing. It is intriguing that in the traditional Greek version of Psalm 96 (95 LXX), the psalm is prefaced by an explanation that offers a dual time reference, reminding us both of David's genius and of a later context when the Temple had been rebuilt after the exile: "When the House was built up after the Captivity, an ode (psalm) of David."

The Rabbis and Tradition

We can see that tradition, in the Jewish context, was simultaneously oral and written. The Psalms, we have seen, were orally and communally recited, but their use was documented and interpreted by the Chronicler, who functions as a scribe by interpreting and passing on the traditional material. Moreover, by the time that we arrive at the turn of the eras, we witness the increased significance of the

1. Kugel, *Traditions of the Bible*, 1.

scribes, or (as they came to be known around the time of Hillel) rabbis ("teachers").[2] Who better to teach the traditions, oral or written, than those who write about them? In order to understand the response of the New Testament to the scribal traditions, it is helpful for us to look at the teachers' assumptions and interpretive principles. In this chapter we will seek to understand the way that the scribes handled tradition, then go on to consider the criticisms leveled at "deadly traditions" (both oral and written) by Jesus and St. Paul, and finally consider why traditions have wrongly been understood as mainly oral by many Christians today.

The work of James Kugel is very helpful in recovering for us the way that the Scriptures were approached at the time when Jesus and the early rabbis were in contact one with the other. At this time, when the rabbis were growing in influence, when Torah was about to take precedence over the Temple (soon to be destroyed), rabbis interpreted the Torah, Prophets, and Writings in such a way that we can discern four assumptions or foundational principles. They believed that the Scriptures were written for the purposes of instruction; they assumed that, despite their various genres and times of composition, the sacred books were harmonious; they engaged in their work because these writings were inspired by God; and they worked hard at their scribal craft because these divine writings, some of them written in the far past, some of them relating divine secrets, were ambiguous, cryptic, or mysterious and required interpretation. In describing the modus operandi of the interpreters, Kugel goes so far as to say that the ancient rabbis assumed that the Bible is fundamentally cryptic and that it speaks indirectly, so that the true sense of a passage is frequently declared to be symbolic and thus really about something that the unlearned reader might never have expected.[3] (We might pause to note that Christians, and in particular Protestants, would applaud the first three assumptions of the rabbis regarding the Bible—its instructive

---

2. It is helpful to distinguish here between priests and scribes: the first concentrated upon the Temple, the second upon the Torah and its interpretation. Of course, the two foci were not mutually exclusive, but when the Temple fell in the late first century AD, the priests (i.e., the Sadducees) no longer had a milieu, whereas the scribes (represented mostly by the Pharisees) came into their own.

3. Kugel, *Traditions of the Bible*, 15.

purpose, inner harmony, and divine inspiration—but vigorously dispute the final assumption, for they have famously championed the perspicuity of Scriptures over its mystery and need to be interpreted by experts.)

Kugel goes on to demonstrate that in their work of interpretation, the rabbis typically paid attention to details, seeming minutiae, but also celebrated the role of wisdom: they were able to see the forest for the trees and to apply the Scriptures in a practical way to life.[4] In looking to the details, they often interpreted difficulties in the text by rewriting or filling in the gaps of the text (the method of "substitution"), so that much of the tradition of the rabbis comes to be found in reworked stories. Such stories do not explicitly call attention to the problems in the original text but paraphrase the text so that what was obscure now makes some sense. In other places, the interpreter actually calls attention to his pedigree, sources, and method, as in the prologue to the Deuterocanonical book of Jesus ben Sirach (known to Western Christians as Ecclesiasticus):

> Whereas many great teachings have been given to us through the law and the prophets and the others that followed them, on account of which we should praise Israel for instruction and wisdom; and since it is necessary not only that the readers themselves should acquire understanding but also that those who love learning should be able to help the outsiders by both speaking and writing, my grandfather Jesus, after devoting himself especially to the reading of the law and the prophets and the other books of our fathers, and after acquiring considerable proficiency in them, was himself also led to write something pertaining to instruction and wisdom, in order that, by becoming conversant with this also, those who love learning should make even greater progress in living according to the law. You are urged therefore to read with good will and attention, and to be indulgent in cases where, despite our diligent labor in translating, we may seem to have rendered some phrases imperfectly. For what was originally expressed in Hebrew does not have exactly the same sense when translated into another language. Not only this work, but even the law itself, the prophecies, and the rest of the books differ not a little as originally expressed. When I came to Egypt in the thirty-eighth year of the reign of Euergetes and stayed for some time, I found

4. Ibid., 19–23.

opportunity for no little instruction. It seemed highly necessary that
I should myself devote some pains and labor to the translation of
the following book, using in that period of time great watchfulness
and skill in order to complete and publish the book for those living
abroad who wished to gain learning, being prepared in character to
live according to the law.

The grandson of ben Sirach here outlines for us in a concise manner the role of the scribe—to be devoted to the Bible, to work with
diligence, to pass on his learning so that others might live in its light,
to translate what might be obscure (despite the inherent difficulties
in translating), and to commend his work to those who are similarly
disposed.

A reading of Sirach will demonstrate the double phenomenon that
we have seen already—respect for tradition coupled with an awareness
of its complexity and its living quality. For example, in speaking about
slaves, seemingly contradictory attitudes of harshness and recognition of them as brothers (Sir. 33:25, 31) are registered. Presumably
the scribe had access to two different traditions regarding slavery and
retained both, cheek by jowl.

As an illustration of the four scribal assumptions, let's consider in a
little more detail, and with the help of Kugel, rabbinic interpretations
of Exodus 15:22–27, where God provides water in the wilderness. In
the sequence of this story, the LORD leads the people from the rescue
scene at the Red Sea into the wilderness, where they are thirsty but
only find bitter water. The people complain, and God shows Moses
a tree, or wood, which he throws into the water, making it sweet. The
LORD then commands them to pay attention to all his words and
commands; if they do this, he will not allow them to be cursed with
diseases like the Egyptians, for he is their healer. After this time of
testing and instruction, they move on to Elim, where they find seventy
palm trees and twelve springs, and encamp by the water.

The mysteries in the text for the rabbis include the connection
between Moses' healing the waters and God's words in the first story,
and the numerological details in the second. It seems a non sequitur,
points out Kugel, that the miracle of healed water is followed by divine
words regarding the commandments and healing from disease: What
is the connection? Further, the informed reader will know that the

numbers twelve and seventy have a traditional value for the Jewish people, recalling the tribes and the elders, or sometimes the number of nations in the world. Those who appreciate the significance of key numbers in the Bible will not be surprised that the details of Elim were interpreted by various rabbis and writers in terms of the twelve tribes and the seventy elders of Israel (cf. Exod. 24:1). Since the text emphasizes the "water," mentioning not simply the springs but also that the Hebrews camped "by the water," and since the sheer number of springs and palms was not remarkable in comparison with what can be found in some fertile places in that area, the rabbis considered that there must be some symbolic importance to mentioning these details. There, Israel was nourished by the water of God—a source for every tribe and expressed in vitality by every elder, or representative of the people. The water, therefore, had to be the very Word of God, which provides life. This is, of course, a meaning that we find in searching the rest of Scriptures—for example, Psalm 1, where the righteous man is portrayed as a tree planted by the waters. Elim, then, came to be seen as an idyllic time when the people, having passed the test at Marah ("he proved them"), paused to meditate upon the commandments. Of course, early Christian interpreters of the text were more likely to interpret the seventy in terms of the nations (also a possible reading in the Hebrew tradition) than in terms of the elders—thus the waters of Elim were intended not only for Israel but also for the nations.

Contemporary readers of this passage will find less natural the symbolic readings of the "wood" that Moses casts into Marah. Here we may be helped by Kugel:[5] readers of the text will wonder why a miracle is followed immediately by God's words regarding obedience and healing. What is the connection between the divine words and the tree in the bitter water? Surely it must be that the tree is something special—a piece miraculously preserved from the tree of life (Pseudo-Philo, *Biblical Antiquities* 11:15), a particular teaching of Torah (Targum Neophyti Exod. 15:25), the Torah itself (Mekhilta Wayyassa' 1), or the basic laws of Torah that dealt with social relations (Babylonian Talmud, *Sanhedrin* 56b). Nor are such allegorical readings

5. Ibid., 615.

found only among the rabbis: in patristic Christian interpretations, the wood of Moses' staff is associated with the Messiah or the cross, and the water with baptism (Tertullian, *On Baptism* 9).

Such symbolic readings seem strained for those of us who have not been trained, as were the rabbis and early Christian interpreters, in a method of interpretation that uses allegory or symbolism where it encounters puzzles. Moreover, we need to remember that such interpretations were natural for those who considered that the whole of Scripture was inspired and that obscure parts could be understood by recourse to other passages (even without respect to their chronological relationship); this strategy has been called "exegetical reciprocity." In the particular case of Exodus 15, the miraculous wood was understood by reference to such verses as Proverbs 3:18, which likens Wisdom (i.e., Torah) to the tree of life. Further, there are in the New Testament certain passages that follow this same procedure, though it seems foreign to those of us who have been informed by what scholars call the historical-critical method. St. Paul, for example, uses what must honestly be called an allegory in speaking about slavery by using the images of Mt. Sinai and Hagar, and about freedom by referring to "the other woman" (Sarah) and "the Jerusalem above" (Gal. 4:26). In a similar vein, he notes without disapproval the tradition, found neither in Exodus 17 nor Numbers 20 but in rabbinic explanations, that the rock that gave water in the desert "followed" the Israelites (literally?), and then he remarks that the rock really was Christ (1 Cor. 10:4). St. Paul, himself a rabbi trained (most probably and surprisingly) both in the Hillel and Shammai schools,[6] did not reject the rabbinic principles of interpretation out of hand but adapted them to his new rule of faith—that the Scriptures point to Jesus.

In the Marah-Elim passage, and the interpretive tradition to which it gave rise, we see all the principles articulated by Kugel: this passage was certainly for instruction, indeed it was about the very source of instruction, the Torah itself; this passage was in harmony with the rest of Scripture, so that one could understand obscure details such as the

6. On Paul's instruction by Gamaliel, a descendant and disciple of Hillel, see Acts 22:3 and Gal. 1:14. On the likelihood that he was also influenced by the more rigorous Shammai school, see Wright, *What St. Paul Really Said*, 26.

wood or water by recourse to other scriptural passages; this passage was divinely inspired and indeed taught that the Torah was inspired; and this passage was mysterious. By paying attention to details such as numbers and the relationship of God's words to the actions of the story, interpreters could, however, move beyond mystification to illumination. Throughout all this, we can see the emphasis upon detail alongside the privileging of wisdom—for, of course, the divine water speaks of God's own wisdom in Torah, and the seventy were frequently associated with the promulgation of wisdom and even the translation of the Hebrew Scriptures into Greek.[7] (This tradition comes over into the New Testament, when Jesus sends out the seventy, after the mission of the Twelve, to proclaim the good news.) Though today's readers may not easily accept the precise symbolic details offered in such readings—indeed, some may find them fanciful—we still should note that the ancient interpreters did not abandon the overall significance of the text—the people were thirsty, and God met their needs, calling them to depend upon him. Their physical need and their spiritual need were intertwined, and both were satisfied by the LORD, who created water and who gave Torah—instruction—to his people.

Here are some of the things that we can glean from our brief visit with the ancient Jewish interpreters. First, the traditions that they pass on do not begin with their own reading of the Scriptures: the rabbis lay hold upon the traditional written material as well as upon traditions of interpretation discernible within the sacred writings themselves.

7. In Jewish legend, seventy translators (of course, not the original seventy elders of the exodus) were said to have simultaneously been inspired to translate the Hebrew Bible into Greek. This story is indicated by the common title given to the fruit of their labor, the Septuagint (LXX), which for a long time was the standard of the Hellenized Jews and came to be the standard Old Testament of the early Christians. It is still considered normative in Orthodox Christianity. Until fairly recently, scholars paid far more attention to the Hebrew Bible that was originally preserved and edited for us by the medieval Jewish scribes known as the Masoretes. Recent finds of ancient Hebrew Old Testament manuscripts in the Dead Sea have shown, however, that sometimes the LXX may preserve for us ancient readings (more "original"?) that were lost to the Masoretes: the relationship, then, between the Masoretic text, the LXX, and earlier lost Hebrew versions appears to be more complicated than once thought. Sometimes the *translated* text may preserve in its meaning something that the Hebrew text that we now have has lost.

Second, tradition is not merely oral but also associated with writing (so that we cannot easily distinguish Scripture as written over against tradition as oral). Third, tradition interprets stories and books that belong in the context of a family or community. Finally, tradition has the force of applying or naturalizing these sacred writings, showing the community how the Scriptures are living and meant for the present time, even where their origins are obscure or their meanings mysterious.

The passing on of tradition is a complex and sometimes messy affair. Standard scholarly accounts of how the central corpus of the Hebrew Bible, the Torah, came to us through its various stages presided over by the elusive Yahwist ("J") of the Southern Kingdom, Elohist ("E") of the North, the Deuteronomist ("D") who was influenced by Josiah's reform, and Priestly ("P") compiler who stressed cultic observances for the people newly returned from exile are probably too simplistic to capture the historical reality. When these theories were first promulgated by German higher critics, the work of P, and even of the redactor ("R") who brought together the strands, were considered to have detracted from the original religious genius of Judaism. In retort, some Jewish scholars have insisted that the letter R for redactor could as well be understood as "Rabbenu"—our rabbi, or teacher, for it is in the lively passing on of the traditions that teaching and reception take place.

In reading the traditional interpretations, there will be points where we worry that tradition has detracted from the original story. (Indeed, as we noted in the previous chapter, we feel such tensions even in comparing parallel stories within the pages of the Bible.) At other times, tradition illuminates or highlights what seemed unimportant in that first telling. At times, the one who passes on the tradition retells, substituting a new version of the story for the first, without calling attention to the changes (as we have seen in the discrepancies between the scriptural stories of David's census). At other times, the traditioner signals what he is doing, as with the grandson of ben Sirach who knew all too well that translation can be misleading, despite the translator's best intentions. With all this in mind, we are now in a better position to understand what the New Testament has to say about tradition, and what in particular Jesus and St. Paul had to say (and did not say) about dead and deadly traditions.

Torah and Tradition in the Gospels

In the first chapter, we noted the influence of Mark 7 and how readings of this passage have predisposed some parts of the Christian community to disparage tradition because it seems that here Jesus gives them cause to do so. However, it is important to read with care, and in entirety, this passage of Jesus' conflict with the Pharisees in order to see all that it has to teach us about tradition. The first thing that we should notice is that with Mark 7 we actually are face-to-face with an example of living Church tradition in the early years of the Church's growth. In fact, the story of Jesus' controversy with the Pharisees concerning washing hands and washing eating vessels is here retold in the context of later Church debate—whether or not Christians can eat nonkosher foods. So the narrator (whether this is Mark or whether he has already received the story with this application) sticks his nose into the midst of telling the story with a parenthetical remark, "In this way, Jesus declared all foods clean" (Mark 7:19 EH). But, of course, in the story itself, Jesus isn't talking specifically about kosher and common foods: he is debating with the Pharisees about whether hands and dishes need to be ceremoniously washed. Mark (or perhaps someone from whom Mark has received the story) has *applied* Jesus' words. This does not mean that we should consider this simply the evangelist's opinion; for Christians, the *interpretation* of Jesus' words in the Gospels is also authoritative. As Fr. Henri de Lubac points out, "The stories that compose our received New Testament, even taking account of the genre representative of each author or the diversity of genres, present themselves to a very large extent as a perpetual interpretation of . . . the Scriptures. This interpretation is . . . in no way like an overlaid embroidery, but it is the very warp and woof."[8] So then, the story about deadly traditions is itself a tradition being passed down to inform a Church that is working through other related and equally difficult matters—debates about table laws and circumcision in the Church that fill up several chapters of Acts and that find their way into Paul's letters to the Galatians, Romans, and Philippians.

8. De Lubac, *L'Écriture dans la tradition*, 22–23, my own translation. De Lubac is speaking specifically about the New Testament interpretation of the Old Testament, but his principle applies also to the New Testament interpretation of Jesus' words.

Moreover, let us look carefully at what Jesus actually says in Mark 7. He does not blame the Pharisees for following in the traditional ways. Rather, he critiques them for not discerning the most serious parts of the Tradition and for following the ways of the elders only *formally* ("with their lips") and not with their heart. Isaiah, whom he quotes, is, after all, part of the prophetic tradition. Jesus further declares that they have "put aside" the commandment of God, while elevating human commandments that originally were intended to *aid* in the keeping of the divine Torah. What the Pharisees call "the tradition of the elders" has been diminished in their hands and been rendered merely "the tradition of men," for the Pharisees are not maintaining a continuity between these traditions and the divine Word. Their problem is not tradition itself, but that they are using lesser traditions for the purpose of eluding the demands of the ongoing Tradition of God.

Indeed, in speaking specifically about the oral traditions followed by the Pharisees (later to be encoded in the Mishnah), Jesus (to the surprise of some) does not challenge them for following these: "But woe to you Pharisees! For you tithe mint and rue and every herb, and neglect justice and the love of God; these you ought to have done, without neglecting the others" (Luke 11:42//Matt. 23:23). We might have said, "These you should ignore, so that you can concentrate more fully upon the greater commands." But, instead, Jesus' argument is one of balance and of giving value to the "weighty matters of Torah" rather than allowing these to be swallowed up by lesser commandments. Even here he does not tell them that they should forgo the added (in his day, oral) commands. He does, however, imply within this discourse that if the *inside* of a person is clean the outside will take care of itself (Luke 11:41//Matt. 23:26). This is an intimation of the new covenant that he would enact, so that the oral protective laws, called by the rabbis "the hedge around the Law," would no longer be necessary. When it becomes possible, by the Spirit and in the new creation, for the believer to have strength inwardly to keep the Law, then it will no longer be necessary to multiply instructions to prevent him or her from breaking it.

In this same passage, Jesus indicts the Pharisees for delighting in the fringes on their prayer shawls and their phylacteries (Matt. 23:5)—the small holy boxes containing bits of God's Word that they wore on their bodies during prayer. Again, these practices were not wrong in themselves. After all, God himself had declared in the Torah that the Law was to be bound on their forehead, placed at their doorways, and so on (Deut. 6:8; 11:18). Whether or not the original intent of the Deuteronomic words was literal, these physical practices were intended to direct people to the Torah, to act as reminders. Moreover, the Torah itself was to act as an usher into God's very own presence. As the Psalmist puts it, "With my whole heart I seek thee; let me not wander from thy commandments! . . . Open my eyes, that I may behold wondrous things out of thy law" (Ps. 119:10, 18; 118:10, 18 LXX).

But, charges Jesus, followed also by St. Paul, there is a stream in Israel that has dropped the search for God and fixated upon the usher (Torah) alone, and upon its decorations (the rabbinic instructions, whether oral or written). For those who do this, the frame has become the center, the door an end in itself. They cannot perceive that the whole of Torah was meant to point to God's greatest treasure of all, Christ, "the end [fulfillment] of the Law," as St. Paul describes him (Rom. 10:4). In speaking of Jesus in this way, the apostle was summarizing what Jesus himself had said when in conflict with those who did not recognize his true identity: "You search the scriptures, because you think that in them you have eternal life; and it is they that bear witness to me; yet you refuse to come to me that you may have life" (John 5:39–40). They were focusing upon the doorposts, upon the container, rather than entering the house or opening the treasure.

The Tradition of Reading Torah and St. Paul

Jesus, St. Paul, and the ensuing Christian way called into question the *manner* in which tradition was valued by the Pharisees, whose movement gave birth to rabbinic Judaism. In forging the identity of a Church gathered around Jesus, the Holy Spirit led Christians to see that they could not center their faith on anything less than the Person who defines all persons: not kosher regulations, not circumcision, not the Temple, not even the Torah. The key identifying mark of the Christian was that he or she was in Christ—this identity does not depreciate the value of the Torah, but it does mean that Torah must keep its proper place, as a pointer to the incarnate LORD.

In Romans, Paul acknowledges that the Law is "holy" and "good" (Rom. 7:1, 12, 14–16), as well as a gift given to the Jews, not to the gentiles. Yet he was concerned for his fellow Jews that they had an unenlightened zeal for God because they did not recognize Jesus (Rom. 10:1–4). What had been a key and necessary part of the life of God's people had not, like the forerunner John the Baptist, been allowed to "decrease" that Christ might "increase" (cf. John 3:30). What had been integral to Judaism was now being allowed to usurp the place of the Messiah (indeed, of God's incarnate, deep visitation of humanity). As a result, the Torah (and its aggregated rabbinic commands) and the rites of the Temple were blocking the view of God's people to where God was leading them: the *means* to intimacy with God had been mistaken for ends in themselves. So Jesus, filled with the Holy Spirit, was condemned for implying that he himself was the true Temple; similarly, the One who was God's righteousness in the flesh was executed as a transgressor of the Law, rather than as One who in his very person fulfilled it.

Indeed, when we look further into St. Paul's comments regarding these matters, we see Paul carefully explaining to the Corinthians that the Law was never meant to be an end in itself and that its glory was meant to be set aside once Jesus, who fulfilled it, was revealed.[9] Both the glory and the provisional quality of the Law should have been recognized through the fact that it actually could do harm, "blind the eyes," whereas when one turns to Christ, any veil is removed. Here it is very

---

9. For those following the RSV, as I myself do most regularly in this study, it is important to recognize that in this rare instance the translators have been themselves misled by a contemporary tradition of interpretation and have wrongly translated 2 Cor. 3:7 as "the Israelites could not look at Moses' face because of its brightness, fading as this was." At some point in the mid-twentieth century, under the influence of such scholars as B. S. Childs, interpreters of 2 Cor. 3 became convinced that there was, at some time, a Jewish legend about the splendor on Moses' face fading, which Paul picks up here to make a theological point. However, no such legend exists, and the stories in Exodus, Numbers, and Deuteronomy have nothing to say about a fading glory. In fact, the verb used in the Greek (*katargein*) does *not* mean "to fade" but "to be set aside, to be demolished." In this passage, then, Paul refers to the glory of the *Torah* as something that was meant to be set aside for its true end or goal—Jesus. Those who focus upon the glory of Torah and do not perceive the greater glory of the LORD, reflected in Moses' face, will miss the real thing. On the debates surrounding this passage see Hays, *Echoes of Scripture*, 133–38.

important to notice that Paul is contrasting the liveliness of those who are in Christ and who are being transformed by the Holy Spirit with the *letter* that "kills" (2 Cor. 3:6). It is not a matter here of criticizing extra oral commandments piled on by the rabbis. Paul, in speaking about the letter that kills, the "ministry of death" (2 Cor. 3:7 NRSV) or "condemnation" (v. 9), is referring to the Torah—*written* documents given by God's angels to Israel—not to scribal oral tradition. The effect of the Torah was to illuminate sin, and its glory was temporary, as can be seen in the fact that it was written upon stones rather than embedded in the human heart. His criticism therefore involves how the rabbis of his day had fixated upon the Hebrew Bible rather than letting it usher them into the very presence of God through Christ.

This unwarranted fixation could either take an academic form that we typically associate with the scribes or be clothed in mystical visionary garb. We see Paul warning the Galatians against the first and more regular form of Torah adulation, where it is clear that Judaizers—Jewish Christians who still insisted upon strict obedience to the Law—have been telling newly converted Christians that they have to submit to circumcision. We very likely see Paul warning against the latter more esoteric "Torahism" in Colossians 2:16–18, where mysterious angelic beings and the commandments are mentioned side by side. Again, in Romans 10:6–8 the apostle rephrases a long-standing tradition about "ascending and descending" to find Torah (Deut. 30:13; Bar. 3:29–30 and other rabbinic writings) with a confident statement that no such visionary excursions are necessary for the Christian since Christ is near.[10] So, then, overconcentration upon the written Word can range from the prosaic and legalistic to emphasis upon spiritual exploits and experience; whether the teacher is didactic or rhapsodic, the problem is the overexaltation of Torah. If the holy text takes first place over God and over Christ, then it has overstepped its role.

10. We have evidence through apocalyptic writings and brief notices in traditional Jewish material that there existed, around the time of Paul and continuing thereafter, a form of mysticism in which rabbis sought to ascend to the throne room of God and grasp the Torah from the hand of the "angel of the Face" who stood at God's right hand. Paul himself may have participated in this mystical rabbinism, for he speaks about having discovered numerous mysteries of God (2 Cor. 12:1–2). For more on Paul and mystical rabbinism, see Humphrey, "Why Bring the Word Down," 129–48.

Is it possible that Christians too can fall prey to a similar danger, forgetting that the whole Bible, including the New Testament, is not an end in itself but functions (can we say?) as an *icon* does, showing us Christ and drawing us into the life of the holy Trinity? There are deadly traditions, and these can be the manner in which we approach *written* as well as *oral* teachings or ideas or practices. That Christian is in danger who concentrates wholly upon a particular view of inspiration, or who forgets that we call the Bible the Word of God because it points to Jesus, the enfleshed, complete, Word of God. Even the Christian who approaches his or her "private time" meditating upon Scriptures as an end in itself could be exposed as hypocritical, open to the charge that Jesus leveled at the Pharisees: one can boast to himself or herself, and not simply in public, and neglect the One to whom devotions are directed! Similarly, someone engaged in spontaneous informal prayer in a prayer meeting might also stop short and value the prayer rather than the One to whom the prayer should point. Deadly tradition is not simply found in formal practices, memorized prayers, or outward practices that can be observed by others; it can be any habit, including a good habit of reading Scripture, which we do not see as a *means* to the one thing necessary—bowing with adoration, along with all those who love the feet of Jesus.

In Jesus' day of corporate identity, the most obvious context for hypocrisy was the public sphere; in our day of privatism and individualism, hypocrisy can easily be nurtured alone. Perhaps, in fact, that is an even more deadly state, because most consider that something done in private is, by that very fact, authentic. The words of the Russian spiritual theologians concerning the general human state of *prelest* (spiritual deception)[11] would be helpful here—it is easy to idolize personal experience, our feelings and passions, and think that we are worshiping God.

Let us return to 2 Corinthians 3 and see how St. Paul used the written traditions of the Hebrew Bible to highlight Jesus, the One to whom all the Law and Prophets and Writings point. The apostle's references to living letters and to the heart do not emerge out of thin

---

11. *Prelest* is discussed by many of those spiritual theologians whose advice to the monks has been collected in *The Philokalia*. See esp. vol. 1.

air, of course. It is clear, from careful attention to his words, that he is recalling the stories of Moses in Exodus and Deuteronomy, as well as the powerful prophecies of Jeremiah 31:31–34 and Ezekiel 36:26–27—tablets of stone, "hearts," "new covenant," "my spirit," and the emphasis upon life. So, then, while recognizing the deadly power of the Law to condemn and to expose, the apostle also turns to the Law and the Prophets to show that the promise of a new covenant was inherent in that collection of sacred texts. The Law had a glory, but it was penultimate, made to guide to something better. The status of the writings by Moses and the prophets was manifest, for these servants had seen God's glory. Yet the time would come when all God's people, not simply their representatives, would have the veil removed and would see God clearly. With great subtlety, and led by the principle that all Scripture points to Jesus, St. Paul reminds us in chapter 3 of these writers of the past and shows how what they had longed for has been fulfilled. Second Corinthians 3 is followed by his fourth chapter, in which he shows that the visitation of the world by Jesus far exceeded the spectacle that Ezekiel had seen on the river Chebar. Ezekiel had glimpsed "the appearance of the likeness of the glory of the LORD" (Ezek. 1:28b) and could thus report to his fellow prisoners that God had not abandoned them in their exile. St. Paul tells the Corinthians (and the Christian community that continues to read his letter) that we have *together* seen "the light of the knowledge of the glory of God in the face of Christ" (2 Cor. 4:6). Together, as a community that reads the Scriptures in the light of Christ, we are seers of God, and the veil is removed. This is a matter of daily life, for we live in the new creation. It is not simply a matter of a single and rare esoteric vision glimpsed occasionally for comfort by one prophet. Moreover, the sight of Christ brings us near to God. As Jesus said, "the one who has seen me has seen the Father" (John 14:9 EH). Beyond that, "all of us together, with unveiled faces, beholding and reflecting the glory of the LORD, are being transformed into that same image, from glory to glory" (2 Cor. 3:18 EH).

So we respect the Scriptures, the wonderful gift that God has given. Though we must acknowledge (as did Jesus and the apostles) that the Torah and the whole of the Old Testament were God's gift to his people, yet we have seen that there is an even greater gift to which all of that was leading. This is, of course, the gift who is Jesus himself and the gift who is the Holy Spirit, come among us to transform us into the divine image ("this comes from the LORD, who is the Spirit" [2 Cor. 3:18 EH]). The personal LORD, and the glory seen in his Church, are the true glory, and so we must take care not to overestimate the role of the written Word, as though knowing the Scriptures were the full goal of the Christian life (though we want to know them!). What characterizes "Christians"—the name given to the disciples at Antioch (Acts 11:26)—is that we are "Christ's ones," *living* letters, God-seers who are daily transformed together into the image of Christ.

Later on in our study, we will consider the relationship between the personal aspect of our faith and living tradition. But for now, let us underscore the way that the New Testament writings themselves do not give undue value to writing over other means of communication. Let us take note of a curious phenomenon at the conclusions of 2 and 3 John. In both of these epistles, the elder ends by saying that there is, in fact, a better way for Christians to speak to each other than the written word: "Though I have much to write to you, I would rather not use paper and ink, but I hope to come to see you and talk with you face to face, so that our joy may be complete" (2 John 1:12); "I had much to write to you, but I would rather not write with pen and ink; I hope to see you soon, and we will talk together face to face" (3 John 13–14). So, then, in its approach to the word, the Bible itself, whether Old Testament or New, does not make a distinction between Scripture and Tradition in terms of what is written over against what is oral. Jesus critiques the Pharisees for neglecting the weightier matters of the Torah, not for having oral traditions. The Torah, Paul suggests, can be used so that it becomes a dead letter or a veil over the face. The elder, writing a letter to his people that will become canonical, points out the importance of face-to-face instruction: indeed, he implies that such communication is even better.

Why Tradition Was Defined as Oral

If we cannot see a firm distinction between oral and written instruction in the New Testament itself, then why is it that so many Christians have come to identify tradition, especially deadly traditions, as mainly oral in nature? This distinction is made not merely by the ordinary Christian but also by academics, who seem to have inherited a perspective that took shape mainly during the debates of the Reformation and Catholic Counter-Reformation. We might consider the excellent essay of New Testament scholar F. F. Bruce,[12] who takes as his point of departure the method of Richard Hooker, that Anglican divine who is usually credited with articulating the "three-legged stool" approach of using Scripture, Tradition, and Reason as authoritative for decision making in the Church. Bruce's description of Hooker's method is masterful, since it sanely places his work within the context of Hooker's own day, while also eschewing an absolute distinction between written Scripture and oral tradition. Nevertheless, this distinction persists, at least in part, even in his well-nuanced essay. In his analysis (oral) tradition retains an importance, but Bruce places this in a decidedly secondary role to (written) Scripture. For example, he insists that the rabbinic teaching that Jesus decried was oral, whereas the originally oral apostolic tradition came to be written down[13]—presumably, the inscribed nature of their witness made it more dependable. In questioning the lines of his argument, we may want to ask, does this mean that the rabbinic teaching, as it came to be written down in the Mishnah, is now authoritative for the Christian? Surely not.

In dealing with early Christian oral tradition, Bruce describes it as having to do mostly with the practicalities of church life. He goes on to comment that Paul "seems to have little interest in questions which have bulked largely in later discussions"[14] concerning, for example, the Eucharist. However, we simply do not know this. It is true that in his discussion of Communion (1 Cor. 11:17–33), St. Paul concentrates on "the fostering of mutual charity,"[15] rather than how one ought to administer the elements. Yet in the same chapter (1 Cor. 11:1–16), the apostle has a good deal to say about such specific things as the covering of women's heads. We know what St. Paul wrote, but we cannot discern from his letters alone what he passed on orally: Can

---

12. Bruce, "Scripture in Relation to Tradition and Reason."
13. Ibid., 37–38.
14. Ibid., 40.
15. Ibid.

we assume that *all* of what Paul considered important found its way into the letters? Probably not, since Paul tells the Corinthians that he has special teaching on wisdom that he teaches to those who are "mature," but he does not divulge this to them in his letter (1 Cor. 2:6–8).

It would seem, then, that the oral tradition to which Paul refers includes more than matters of mere practicality and comprises ways of piety, family stories about God's people, and such glimpses of glory that St. Paul (and others) passed on to their spiritual "children." Bruce acknowledges that there was "at first no distinction in principle between Christian tradition and Christian Scripture,"[16] but then says that by the end of the second century "it seems clear . . . that by [t]his time not much more was available than the last scrapings from the barrel of oral tradition."[17] This conclusion is not so very clear, however. Bishop Papias, whom Bruce is quoting, preferred to listen personally to the disciples of the apostles rather than read the memoirs. But this does not mean that oral tradition had misfired and that it was no longer available from the mouths of those who heard those who knew the apostles, including Papias himself. We need to consider the probability, for example, that oral tradition played a key role in the later development of Christology and Eucharistic theology—surely there are intimations of this process in passages such as 1 Corinthians 11:23 and John 6:32–58.[18] Clearly, one very important oral tradition continued to be transmitted: how the Scriptures of the Old Testament were to be interpreted, as pointing forward to Christ.

And so we are helped by Bruce's candid admission of the fact that the Scriptures themselves came out of traditions and then were interpreted, within Israel and within the Church, by tradition. The most clear and unique conviction of early Christians was that they insisted upon "finding Christ in all the Scriptures"—a method delivered, suggests F. F. Bruce (and Luke 23:27), by Jesus himself and passed on by the apostles to the early Church fathers.[19] Here is a tradition of interpreting the Old Testament that is passed down orally: it is mentioned by Luke, or in Hebrews 1:1, but not described in detail.

16. Ibid., 38.
17. Ibid.
18. I am indebted to conversations with the Rev. Dr. John Breck for this suggestion.
19. Bruce, "Scripture in Relation to Tradition and Reason," 48.

We can *see* the New Testament writers and the fathers engaging in this procedure, but we are not privy to the apostolic instruction as to how it ought to be done in the New Testament itself. Later in this book we will consider some of the teachings of St. Irenaeus (second century) concerning how Christian interpretation differed from Gnostic interpretation of the Old Testament. In his instruction, we can discern some of the principles that were passed on.

With all this in mind, we must then continue to ask, is the oral/written distinction a valid way of determining what is vital for the Church and what is not? Hooker himself, who made this distinction, wrote with the Reformation debates very much in mind. The acute debates between Protestants and Catholics at that time came to be framed in terms of the commendation of Tradition by Catholics and an attack upon many Church traditions as superfluous and even enslaving by Protestants. In reaction to Protestants who were declaring that the Bible alone was authoritative, the Roman Catholic Council of Trent (1546), in its fourth session, issued this decree:

> This [Gospel], of old promised through the Prophets in the Holy Scriptures, our Lord Jesus Christ, the Son of God, promulgated first with His own mouth, and then commanded it to be preached by His Apostles to every creature as the source at once of all saving truth and rules of conduct.
>
> It [the Church] also clearly perceives that these truths and rules are contained in the written books and in the unwritten traditions, which, received by the Apostles from the mouth of Christ Himself, or from the Apostles themselves, the Holy Ghost dictating, have come down to us, transmitted as it were from hand to hand.
>
> Following, then, the examples of the orthodox Fathers, it receives and venerates with a feeling of piety and reverence all the books both of the Old and New Testaments, since one God is the author of both; also the traditions, whether they relate to faith or to morals, as having been dictated either orally by Christ or by the Holy Ghost, and preserved in the Catholic Church in unbroken succession.[20]

This preamble is followed by an enumeration of the canonical books (including the Deuterocanonical or Apocryphal books) and by strict

---

20. The text is available at http://www.ewtn.com/library/councils/trent4.htm. Accessed January 2012.

regulations concerning how these books were to be promulgated only in the approved translation (the old Latin Vulgate). Further, teaching from the Scripture needed to be approved by the bishops, so that it conformed to the historical teaching of the Church and to what the medieval Catholics believed was the unanimous teaching[21] of the Church fathers. These measures, intended to repress "profane" or incorrect interpretation, were to be enforced by canon law, including the penalties of fines and even anathema.

In this war cry against what was perceived to be radical and disruptive Protestantism, the decree itself makes the distinction between Scripture and Tradition in terms of what is written and what remains unwritten—and so the Council of Trent sets the terms for the debate between Catholicism and Protestantism in these matters. The suggested original draft for this declaration was that truth was to be found "partly" in Scripture and "partly" in Tradition. This *"partim . . . partim"* teaching did not find its way into the final text,[22] as can be seen, yet the Trent documents are usually interpreted as implying this relationship. Catholics, then, see Scripture (written) and Tradition (oral) as mutually informing one another and as both necessary to understand the Gospel. Protestants, stressing the importance of the written Word, and in great reaction to what were seen as repressive measures (the control of printing and preaching under pain of excommunication), naturally pushed back and rejected oral tradition. In particular, Protestants deplored the tradition that the Church hierarchy is the arbiter of "true sense and interpretation." Today, most Protestant scholars are considered worth reading if they bring "fresh readings" and novel interpretations to the text, not if they continue to read according to the "unanimous teaching of the Fathers" (the

---

21. A scholastic belief in such patristic unanimity has not always been the approach of the Orthodox Church to the witness of the fathers. Many prefer to speak about the "mind of the Church," instead, without implying absolute confluence in every area of thought. The fathers, as faithful interpreters responding to the mysteries that have been revealed, also formulate *theologoumena*, that is, pious theological opinions.

22. On this, see Joseph Ratzinger (Pope Benedict XVI), *God's Word*, 48. The pope here takes up the discussion of R. Geiselmann, *Die Heilige Schrift und Die Tradition* (1962), agreeing with Geiselmann's observations regarding the first draft of the decrees but disagreeing with his conclusion that a faithful Catholic could take up a *sola Scriptura* position.

wording of the Decree of Trent). Indeed, most Protestants are embarrassed by the methods normatively followed by the early fathers. Most would never consider that such practices were in continuity (at least in part) with the rabbinic ways of reading and that these methods had been passed down, with a particular Christian shape, by the apostles or by Christ himself. The weight the Catholic Church placed upon tradition—including the long-standing emphasis upon winning merit with God by cultic practices, the selling and buying of indulgences, the top-down governance of the Church—was part and parcel of the Reformers' critique of Rome. Trent's appeal to traditional interpretation as the arbiter of Scriptures (including allowing the Scriptures only in Latin) was a further irritant for those Protestants who saw such measures as obscuring the meaning of the Gospel rather than preserving it. Tradition was the main culprit, and that tradition was seen as oral.

Removing the Stigma

Tradition, then, is a dirty word for Protestants, while essential for Roman Catholics. Connotations of words cloud over their primary meaning. I could not call my daughter "Penelope," no matter how mellifluous the sound of that name, if the only Penelope I knew as a child looked like one of Cinderella's stepsisters. It is just that difficult for freedom-loving Protestant Americans to think positively about tradition. Further, Christians who value Tradition tend to think of it in terms of oral teaching rather than written. Yet so much of the historic Church's Tradition (creeds, liturgy, hymnody, classical prayers, canon law) is *written*! Very few consider the role of Tradition to go beyond doctrine and morals (those two areas highlighted by Trent), nor do they appreciate how Tradition gives rise to personal formation and vibrant Church life. How, then, can we remove the stigma, confusion, and constraints associated with the word and illuminate Tradition in its true colors, so that its beauty and dynamism can be appreciated? Already we have taken note of the *particular* critique that Jesus had of the Pharisaic tradition, that same criticism St. Paul leveled against the Judaizers: they concentrated upon the elder's precepts or upon

Torah as ends in themselves rather than as lively means to the living God. As Jesus described them, "The scribes and the Pharisees sit on Moses' seat" (Matt. 23:2) but were not demonstrating by their actions that Moses had brought them any closer to God. In the next chapter, we will go forward to look at how St. Paul and the early apostles (some of them Pharisees with a new focus!) operated within the living Tradition of the Church as they helped to resolve confusions and problems and as they sought to guide the believing communities into the fullness of life and truth, centered upon the Lord.

ー3ー

THE APOSTLES, THE WORD,
AND THE LETTER

For it has seemed good to the Holy Spirit and to us . . . to the apostles
and the elders, with the whole church . . . and with this the words of
the Prophets agree . . . (Acts 15:28, 22, 15)

So far in our study, we have recalled the mixed response that tradition
elicits in our day, considered some of the debates among Christians
surrounding the relationship between tradition and Scripture, and
noted the critique of both Jesus (as seen in the Gospels) and St. Paul
as they faced Pharisaic/rabbinic approaches to tradition and interpretation of the Hebrew Bible. Though we briefly have observed both
similarities and differences between traditional Jewish approaches
and the perspective of early Christian writers, we have not had an
opportunity to look in detail at the apostles' stance (as seen in the
New Testament) toward tradition. This chapter, then, is the "meat and
potatoes" course for our study in the biblical foundations for Christian
tradition as a key element of the faith. In this chapter, we will begin
with the reflection upon tradition that we find in 2 Peter, continue
with a pivotal example reported to us by Luke in his second volume,

the Acts (chapters 10–16), and then move on to a debated passage in Paul's letter to the Galatians. There we will see that a careful reading of Paul's words to the Galatians will correct the (mis)understanding that some contemporary interpreters have made popular, in which they assert that he depended only upon personal revelatory experience while disdaining both authority and tradition. We will then conclude by collecting other various passages in his letters where Paul turns to tradition in dealing with a host of topics, including worship, the practice of the Lord's Supper, and human nature (2 Thessalonians and 1 Cor. 11). In all this, we will see how tradition was an essential element in the life of the early Church, so that the earliest teachers of the Church even engaged in reflection upon the relationship between Scripture, personal revelation, and tradition.

Apostolic Witness: A Lamp Shining

The Second Letter of Peter speaks specifically about how the Christian life is nurtured by revelation (both personal and mediated), written Scripture, and tradition (whether oral or written). The letter recalls with wonder the revelation of the divine Son on the Mount of Transfiguration. Remembering that One who received (*paralambanō*, 1:17) glory from the Father, the apostle[1] writes:

1. Contemporary scholarly opinion does not generally accept 2 Peter as from the pen of Simon Peter. No doubt one of the reasons for this is its careful reflection upon matters such as tradition and revelation, topics that some think would not have been treated with care in the Church until a generation subsequent to the first apostles. Moreover, the Greek in this epistle is quite polished, rather similar to that of Luke's Gospel. It is important to remember that authorship of letters was not necessarily a solo matter: frequently in Paul's letters, multiple authorship is documented in the initial greetings, and the convention of using an amanuensis (sometimes with pretty free rein, going beyond mere transcription) was common. The debate concerning whether or not early Christians accepted with ease letters written under pseudonyms is ongoing. In the case of 2 Peter, this suggestion of a convention that acknowledged pseudepigraphy is difficult, at least from the perspective of those who see the book as Scripture. This is because the epistle actually appeals to an eyewitness experience of the Transfiguration as the basis of its authority and truthfulness. However, the letter can be said to be apostolic, rather than merely pseudepigraphical, even if the actual hand of Peter did not pen these words, if the burden of its argument came originally from Peter and was licked into shape by a disciple who was instructed in

And we have (established as) more secure the prophetic word. To this you will do well to pay attention, as to a lamp shining in a dark place, until the day dawns and the morning star rises in your hearts. In the first place, you must understand that no prophecy of Scripture opens itself automatically to interpretation, because no prophecy ever came by human will; but holy human beings, moved by the Holy Spirit, spoke from God. (2 Pet. 1:19–21 EH)

Notice the way in which the apostle shows the Christian family as knit together, interconnected. He tells his readers that we have the prophetic word made "more firm" because of the revelation of Jesus' glory among the apostles who saw and heard the Lord on a daily basis, from his obscure beginnings as a teacher to his public notoriety, and because of their sure witness to his cross, resurrection, and ascension. The line of reception from Jesus to apostles to Church is clear—yet the final recipients are not described as under a borrowed light, for the lamp is theirs!

Because the Church is one body, past and present, the witness of the apostles shines as a "lamp," a luminary dependent upon the promised Morning Star who comes—Jesus himself. The initiative comes from One who is the Logos and has entered into our world: assurance is given to the Church because he visited us deeply in the Incarnation; hope is given to the Church because he has promised to return in full glory. The One who is the Word is intimately interconnected, then, with the prophets who foresaw him and even more directly with the apostles who saw and proclaimed him. And the witness of the prophets, confirmed through the sight of Jesus by the apostles, is God's gift to the Church through the ages.

This transmission and reception is not a graded chain of communication with the danger of a weak link, as in the game of "broken-telephone." Though the lamp comes from the apostolic witness, the light shines upon every member of the Church, and the handling of Scriptures itself takes place in the context of God's people, not merely

---

his traditional teaching. A particularly illuminating discussion of this issue has most recently been joined by Bauckham, *Jude and 2 Peter*. We will not entertain the debate at this point, but receive the letter as in at least some sense apostolic, following the decision of the Church to include it in the list of books that were "canonical"—according to the rule of faith.

by means of certain privileged Church leaders. (Of course, we need to remember that in the case of this early letter, "every Scripture" refers to the Old Testament books, which, the apostles taught, all spoke of Jesus.) Just as revelation from God did not come to one person alone, so implies 2 Peter, it is never interpreted by an individual alone. Rather, the Holy Spirit spoke God's Word to human beings (plural), and in the same manner the Church together reads, interprets, and receives the Scriptures as pointing to Christ. "To *this*—to the Scriptures made sure through the apostolic witness—you will do well to pay attention" (2 Pet. 1:19 EH), he declares.

These oracles of God are, moreover, not "self-interpreting" (this is the literal meaning of the Greek text in verse 20). That is, they do not open their deepest meaning just automatically to anybody. Rather, the revealed words of God come clear in the light of Christ and in the context of the community that has understood how the Old Testament points to him, the One whom they worship. We pause to notice that the Petrine teaching does not agree exactly with the rabbis, who considered that the Scriptures were wholly obscure and required specialists to interpret; neither does it agree fully with Protestant egalitarian optimism that the words of Scripture are entirely obvious to whomever reads them off the page. The mystery has been dispelled in the light of Christ, but it continues to be communicated through those who are in Christ; for example, the Ethiopian official implied to Philip that he could not understand Isaiah 53 without Philip's insight. From beginning to end, God the Holy Spirit works within the community of faith; God the Father bears witness to the Son, in the sight and hearing of the apostles. The apostles, taught by Jesus, show how the words of the Hebrew prophets have been fulfilled in Christ, and they interpret these words together with the whole community. The Holy Spirit breathes life and inspired words into holy men and women (*anthropoi*, 2 Pet. 1:21), who speak in harmony with all that God has said and who illumine what God wants the Church to see.

So, then, the epistle of 2 Peter speaks about the living tradition of God's Word, both spoken ("we heard the voice on the mountain") and written ("prophecy of Scripture"), communicated from persons to persons. This tradition is not simply about faith and morals, nor about worldviews and ideas, though it is interconnected with these. Like the episode of the Transfiguration it is focused upon Jesus himself, the One who is the Word, the One who has been given over to us as a priceless gift by the Father. In a similar way, the preface to the Hebrews joins God's spoken and written Word with the One who is the Word: "In many and various ways God spoke of old to our fathers by the prophets; but in these last days he has spoken to us by a Son, whom he appointed the heir of all things" (Heb. 1:1–2). Again, in harmony with Hebrews and 2 Peter, St. Paul tries to move the Corinthians beyond an infant faith and asks them,

> For what person knows those things that pertain to a human being except the spirit of the human that is in him? So also no one comprehends the thoughts of God except the Spirit of God. Now we have received not the spirit of the world, but the Spirit who is from God, that we might understand the gifts bestowed on us by God. And we impart this in words not taught by human wisdom but taught by the Spirit, interpreting spiritual truths to those who possess the Spirit. (1 Cor. 2:11–13 EH)

Some have read the "we" here as simply a royal we, a plural signifying the author. Instead, I think, we should understand the "we" and "us" of 2 Peter 1, Hebrews 1, and 1 Corinthians 2 as the communal "we"—apostolic insights that have been clarified and passed on in the Christian community. In all this, the verbal word, the written word, and Jesus the Word come together, imparted internally among and within the community. To understand the revelation of God involves the vivifying power of the Holy Spirit within those who are teaching such mysteries and within those who are receiving them. Reception is not a private matter, but it is at once personal and communal, pertaining to the "spirit" in each person and pertaining also to the "Spirit" who has been imparted to each as well as to the body of believers. Paul also, let us recall, commended his followers for paying attention to the traditions (*paradoseis*) that they had received from him, whether by letter or by word (2 Thess. 2:15). Like Peter and Hebrews, he made no strict distinction between letter and spoken word, nor did subsequent generations of Christians, it seems. All of these words are gifts from God to the Church and to those within the Church, and they give life.

As 1 Peter puts it, because of Jesus, "the living stone" we are "living stones" "built into a spiritual house" (1 Pet. 2:5) and offering back to God all things that have been given to us. This aspect of interconnection is seen in our teaching, in our life together, in our worship, in our prayers for each other, in our witness to others, and in our dwelling as a single body, brothers and sisters, present and past. Consider that little vignette of the early Church given by Luke in Acts 2: the early disciples "gave themselves to the teaching of the apostles and to the communion of the apostles" (EH). Luke even paints for us a word picture here, placing the word "of the apostles" between the words for teaching and communion.

They gave themselves . . .

to the teaching ⟶ *of the apostles* ⟵ *and to the communion.*

It was not simply that the early Christians gave mental assent to a body of doctrine that the apostles had borrowed from Jesus and consolidated. No, they attached themselves to the apostles and to each other and so learned about life, faith, and worship, Jesus-style. If we do not take account of the living quality of our faith, but reduce it to sheer philosophy, morals, or doctrine (though these things are important), we may well get things distorted. Remember the warning in 2 Peter concerning those parts in Paul's letters that were "hard to understand" and misread by unstable teachers (2 Pet. 3:14–18).

Let us go on, then, to see how the apostles, whom Jesus established in the early Church, and the elders, whom the apostles appointed, made decisions with and for the early Church on the basis of spoken words, the Word of Scripture, and the illumination of the Holy Spirit. Clearly, the early Church faced decisions just as difficult as those that we face today. When this happened, the apostles and teachers did not contemplate that the word of the Holy Spirit could be in a collision course with how God had acted in the past. We see this in the bracing story of Acts 10–11 (and its sequel in Acts 15), which emphasizes for us the roles of Tradition and Scripture as foundational for decision making in the Church.

Authority, Agency, and Action in the Church

This story is told quite wonderfully by Luke, a master storyteller. Most Christians remember one of its main highlights: Peter's vision of the sheet filled with nonkosher animals that he is told three times to eat. But besides this vision, there are also: Cornelius' matching vision of Peter coming to see him; Peter's actual visit to the household of the gentile Cornelius; the stirring oration that Peter gives when the household is assembled; the climax when Cornelius, with his household, are converted and filled with the Spirit; and the ensuing debate about eating with gentile believers that was resolved among the apostles in Jerusalem.

The first thing to notice is that the story is not simply about a principle or a new way of life—it is about the life of the Church together. We might be tempted to think that Peter's vision concerns what Christians may or may not eat. It actually doesn't (though that issue may be involved). The animals in Peter's vision pointed to those whom the Torah had declared "common" or "unclean"—gentiles who were not able, under the Old Covenant, to be part of God's people unless circumcised. So, then, though food and table regulations are involved, the story is primarily about the Word of God being proclaimed among gentiles—among those whom God has, by Jesus' visitation of the world, proclaimed "clean." The story is replete with instances of communion—emissaries from Cornelius come to Peter, Peter with three others goes to Cornelius and his family, Peter meets with the apostles in Jerusalem. Peter preaches a sermon centered upon Jesus, the One who makes communion possible, and refers in it to the Old Testament prophets who bore witness to the Christ to come. The Holy Spirit, that One who joins us together in the Church, visits and fills the members of Cornelius' household. Peter rejoices with them and must then explain this astounding episode to the rest of the Church, with whom he is "in communion" and who are worried about whether Peter, by consorting with Gentiles, has acted unlaw-. fully, against the Torah.

Second, the revelation of the Lord is not portrayed in this story as "self-interpreting," nor as "opening itself automatically to interpretation" (2 Pet. 1:20 EH). God uses a double-vision strategy:

complementary things, things that fit together, are shown to more than one person. While the Spirit is speaking to Cornelius, he is also prompting Peter. Now of course this is a famous strategy in ancient literature that is being used by Luke (who was an educated author). But it isn't just a strategy—it is also a sign of how God works. This is underscored both in the narrative and in the double vision. The twin visions that Peter and Cornelius receive are told again and again to make up a total of five vision reports before Peter actually preaches. These reports come to a climax in Peter's missionary sermon, where he explains what God has shown him. Finally, the visions are again rehearsed as Peter defends himself and helps the believers (and their leaders) in Jerusalem to understand.

We are not privatized individuals in the Church. "It is not good for man to be alone" was God's first word of critique at the dawn of creation. This is not just a principle of who we are but also of how we are to understand the movement of the Holy Spirit and (by extension) the Bible. The very structure of this narrative—people hearing words from God, seeing visions, bringing these together for understanding, and then ratifying the whole within a Church assembly—shows how God works among *us*, not just in the imagination of one charismatic leader (Peter), or in the opinion of biblical specialists ("the circumcision party," 11:2), nor even in the solemn judgment of the official leader (James, as we see when the topic is revisited in chapter 15). This emphasis upon the "us" is actually problematic for me as a scholar, in this day when, in academic as well as popular circles, "fresh readings" are appreciated! How can those of us who value tradition gain a hearing in a day when ears are itching for novelty? The answer is, of course, that people have so forgotten the Great Tradition that they often think it is something new when they hear it for the first time. I remember being amused with the enthusiasm of a woman in my class for what she thought was a new way of interpreting a passage—it actually had come from St. John Chrysostom, but I had been pressed for time and hadn't added a verbal footnote. Of course, when the Holy Spirit speaks, it is always "fresh," even though it may not be "new."

This leads us into our third point. The vision of Peter is not some brand-new revelation that has no connection with the gospel. The story comes to its climax as Peter proclaims Jesus and as the gentiles receive the Holy Spirit. Indeed, what happens to them (Acts 10:44–48) is completely in harmony with what God has been doing in the Church, for the gentiles are immediately baptized in the name of Jesus Christ. Moreover, Peter's sermon makes clear that what is happening under the new covenant is not an abrogation or canceling of Torah (not "unlawful," cf. 10:28) but its fulfillment. As he speaks to the gentile household (whose head was a God-fearer, one who knew the Hebrew Scriptures), Peter appeals to the prophets, relating the gospel in language that recalls the Hebrew Bible ("third day," 10:40; "judge of the living and the dead," 10:42), and ending in this way: "To him [Jesus] all the prophets bear witness that everyone who believes in him receives forgiveness of sins through his name" (10:43). The baptism of these gentiles, then, is the fulfillment of prophetic words that declared "in his name shall the nations hope" (Isa. 42:4 LXX[2]; Matt. 12:20–21 EH). As Vladimir Lossky points out, the Law is interpreted *through* the prophets by the early Church, showing us the principle of ongoing Tradition even within the Scriptures themselves:

> A written obligation to which the chosen people must submit, the Law is accompanied by divine promises that the Prophets will continue to make precise. Thus the Law and the Prophets complement each other; and Christ will always evoke them together. The Prophets are the men whom God chose to announce the profound meaning of His Law. . . . The Prophets, in their relationship to the chosen people . . . play an analogous role to that of Tradition in the Church: Prophets and Tradition in fact show us the real meaning of the Scriptures. And the duality of Law-Prophets already expresses . . . the defining action of the Logos and the life-giving action of the Holy Spirit. In the Old Testament in fact the spirit of prophecy makes us perceive clearly the action of the third person of the Trinity.[3]

2. Note that the Greek version (LXX or Septuagint) here diverges from the Hebrew, which speaks merely of the coast-people, not of the gentiles specifically. The early Church received the LXX, originally a Jewish version, by tradition, and many of the allusions or citations of the New Testament are to this version, which favors a Christian interpretation. This is not the place to discuss accuracy, but it should be noted (see chapter 2, note 7) that we cannot necessarily assume that the Hebrew editions of the Bible to which we have access through the Masoretic scribes are always closest to the "original" or most ancient editions (now lost to us) simply because they are in Hebrew.

3. Lossky, *Orthodox Theology*, 88–89.

So, then, the immediate present action of the Holy Spirit is not completely novel but coheres with the promises of the prophets, both that
God should refresh Israel and that the nations or gentiles would also
be involved. The coming together of Cornelius and his household
with the apostle Peter makes this a kind of twin Pentecost for the
gentiles, to be interpreted as the apostles had interpreted the events
of Acts 2—by the Hebrew prophets and in the light of Jesus.

Remember, Peter was the apostle who had witnessed to the Jews
gathered in Jerusalem on that first giving of the Spirit. Now he witnesses to the gentiles and observes what the Holy Spirit does among
them, so that he can explain to the rest of his colleagues what God is
doing. He will tell his fellow apostles that, in response to his preaching
of the gospel, the gentiles have begun to speak God's very Word and
to praise God (Acts 10:46). The life, ministry, death, resurrection, and
ascension of Jesus has issued in an apostolic Church that has power
to proclaim God's Word and that grows because together believers
come to know the One who is the Word. *All* this is centered around
Jesus—*not* around the mystical vision of Peter, nor the worthiness of
Cornelius, nor the boldness of the apostles. What is happening honors
the Lord Jesus and raises him up, helping more and more voices to
swell the chorus of those who tell the truth with joy.

Look also at how the meaning of the visions unfolds naturally in
the story's action. It isn't a matter of someone seeing a vision and
cleverly figuring out what it means. Rather, Peter follows God's directions step-by-step, as does Cornelius, as do the disciples in chapter 11,
and God's meaning becomes clear. This is different from some kinds
of visionary literature such as, for example, many of those strange
books that we call apocalypses. So naturally do the interpretations
come in Acts that we hardly notice them: "Do not call unclean what
God has cleansed," "I now understand that God shows no partiality,"
"everyone who believes in him receives forgiveness," "The Spirit told
me . . . not to make a distinction," "So then, God has given even to the
gentiles repentance that leads to life"(10:15, 34; 11:12, 18 EH). The
whole thing unfolds like a living tree, and we are drawn into the story.
There is no sense of an esoteric vision or mystery being "decoded" by
an expert. Though the community is in view, the apostolic position
of Peter and the others is also important—for they can recognize

Jesus' style of operation. Yet the whole Church is in this together, including the newcomers.

Look also at how many times in the story people pray: in 10:2 Cornelius prays; in 10:4 the angel speaks about Cornelius praying; in 10:9 Peter prays; in chapter 11 Peter explains about how he was praying; and once the assembly in Jerusalem has heard about the whole thing, they stop attacking Peter and praise God. Chapter 11 begins by Jewish Christians questioning "Did Peter break the law?" It ends with an understanding that, through Peter, God has begun the mission to the gentiles: "So then, to the Gentiles, God has also granted repentance unto life" (11:18 EH). The issue of unlawful entry into Cornelius' house (because Peter is Jewish) is replaced by the issue of gentile homes being united to the household of God. The whole assembly comes to understand this because they are thinking things through together, by prayer, by reference to what they know of the Lord Jesus, and by listening to how the Holy Spirit has acted in harmony with the Gospel. The Church's decision is made by seeking the face of God.

We have seen, then, that God speaks to several people in ways that harmonize. Next, we've seen that what he says and shows is intimately connected with the Lord Jesus, consistent with the gospel, consistent with the Hebrew Scriptures as interpreted by the prophets, and discerned by the whole Church in the context of prayer. Further, we've seen that it isn't a matter of being skilled in figuring out what God wants, or in forcing the evidence to go in a certain way: there is no certain privileged person being given *the* interpretation to pass on to others. The Church sees this unfold and interprets the meaning together, with the leaders finally acknowledging together what has been learned. Peter gives them the warrants of his vision, Cornelius' vision, and what he has remembered from Jesus' teaching:

> "And I remembered the word of the Lord, how he said, 'John baptized with water, but you shall be baptized with the Holy Spirit.' If then God gave the same gift to them as he gave to us when we believed in the Lord Jesus Christ, who was I that I could withstand God?" When they heard this they were silenced. And they glorified God, saying, "Then to the Gentiles also God has granted repentance unto life." (Acts 11:16–18)

The apostles, then, learn together with the gentiles. They recall
Jesus' own words and they heed what God is doing among them: in the
words of Fr. John Breck, "Tradition is actualized through *anamnesis*
(memory)."[4] They retain their special role, for they have been with
Jesus and they know his style of ministry—that is, his way of calling
to repentance, his manner of cleansing and healing. They look back to
the tradition of Jesus' words and see its consonance with the present
action of God, surprising though that may seem to them. Cornelius
saw in his vision an angel, an emissary of God, *entering* into his
house—this angelic action is repeated by Peter in his apostolic entrance into the gentile world. Nor is this the last debate on the subject.
Again, in chapter 15, the circumcision party that had accused Peter
"You went in and ate with Gentiles!" (11:3 EH) is troubling gentile
converts around the civilized world by claiming that the apostles at
Jerusalem were imposing circumcision upon these believers. When
Paul and Barnabas go to check out the report at Jerusalem, some of
the circumcisers stand up in council to make similar demands.

The result is a general meeting of the apostles and the elders, who,
after "much debate," listen to Peter, who recalls for them the events
with Cornelius and the decision taken then. He reminds them that it
is the Holy Spirit and not the Torah that cleanses, and that the Torah
has been, at any rate, imperfectly kept by the people of Israel. Then
Paul and Barnabas give witness to what has been going on among the
gentile churches abroad. Finally, James, the leader in Jerusalem, who
has been silent to this point, sums up what they have learned: already
the problem of the gentiles has been examined through the encounter
of Peter with Cornelius, already they have seen that the prophets
pointed forward to the cleansing of the gentiles. On the basis of all
that they have learned, he gives a judgment, saying that the gentile
God-fearers will know the basic laws of Torah (no sexual immorality,
no idolatry, and no eating of blood or what has been strangled): only
these should be required, so that Jewish and gentile believers can be
at harmony with each other. Though James gives the word, it is clear
that he is drawing upon the past decisions the apostles have made

4. This was Fr. Breck's comment to me in private conversation, but the principle
can be seen also in his *Scripture in Tradition*, inter alia 12, 226.

together. Moreover, his word is ratified by all those present, who send emissaries (Jude and Silas) with Paul and Barnabas back to the congregations that have been troubled. They bring a message in which they say that they are in agreement (15:25), and that the decision is one that "seemed good to the Holy Spirit and to us" (Acts 15:28).

By this long and two-step learning experience, the Church resolves the nature of its new identity, Jew and gentile together trusting in Jesus, the One for whom the Torah prepared and the One to whom the prophets, interpreting the Torah, pointed. (Notice that the decision taken in chapter 11 is revisited and ratified in chapter 15, and will in chapter 16 be received by the faithful. This is a pattern of decision making that the ecumenical Church of the first five centuries will follow in the establishing of the creeds.) Numerous gentiles enter into the household of God, a movement that fulfils even what Abraham (in the Torah) had been told—that by his seed would "the whole world be blessed."

These controversies took some time to work out, but in the end, both written-word and word-of-mouth teachings helped to interpret the events of the present day and were confirmed by the Spirit among the believers (Acts 15:28). The Holy Spirit used the leaders, the missionaries, and the rest of the faithful to confirm and reaffirm these decisions:

> As they went on their way through the cities, they made it a practice to "tradition" (*paradidōmi*) the teachings that had been discerned by the apostles and elders who were at Jerusalem so that they would be guarded (by the new believers). In this way, the churches were being strengthened in the faith, and they increased in numbers daily. (Acts 16:4–5 EH)

Those with keen ears will note the closing cadence and its parallel to the beginning of the Church when, after Pentecost, "the Lord added daily to their number those who were being saved" (2:47 EH). The picture is that of a single tree growing in a consistent manner in all parts and interconnected in every way. It is a single spiritual organism, joined across both geographical and temporal distance with the apostles and elders in Jerusalem. They "deliver" to the new believers that which the apostles and elders had to give, and so the Church grows and is strengthened. Its strength lies in the delivered and received tradition, a tradition that ensures the vitality of the Church.

Spoken Word, Scripture, and Personal Instruction in Paul's Letters

There are, of course, some scholars who would query the pattern offered in Acts. Is this happy story due to Luke's desire for decency and order, so that he ends up with a certain compromising position between those who insisted upon Jewish ways and those who preached the Torah-free Pauline gospel? Some scholars have been suspicious of Luke's narrative and have suggested a way of tracing the history of early Church practice and teaching in terms of a thesis-antithesis-synthesis model. In this historical reconstruction, Paul's free and dynamic gospel, as preached among the Gentiles, is countered violently by a pro-Torah party of Jerusalem Christians, causing initial conflict in the early era of Christianity. A final stage, a synthesis, emerges, which Luke is said to have read back into the turbulent days of the Church when he wrote the book of Acts. This synthesis was dubbed "early Catholicism"— and "Catholicism" is not here intended as complimentary but as a compromise that diminished the original Christian freedom. In this representation of things, made popular by F. C. Baur and the "Tübingen school," St. Paul is depicted as a kind of "lone ranger" apostle who bravely and freely contradicted the apostles of Jerusalem, because they had difficulty getting beyond Jewish enslavement to rules, whereas he had been directly called by the Spirit of God. Paul's communities were originally totally free of regulation, they say, and then due to Luke and others who followed after Paul's day, these Jesus communities hardened into a more hierarchical institution.

But a careful look at Paul's own letters shows that this scheme (Pauline libertarians opposed by rigid Jewish Christians, and then the emergence of a compromise, "early Catholicism") is hardly the case. In Galatians, that very letter where Paul stands firm against those who would impose Jewish practices like circumcision upon the Church, Paul actually defers to the principles of both personal responsibility and authority in the Church. Let us read the passages in question (Gal. 1:11–2:10) to make this clear.

To be sure, Paul says that he is an apostle "not by or through humans" (Gal. 1:1 EH) and he emphasizes that he received his commission from the Lord Jesus himself—probably because those who were detracting from his mission gave their own pedigrees as coming "from James" and other apostles. Indeed, some have seen Galatians 2:12, "certain men came from James," to be in direct opposition to the words of Acts 15:24, where the apostles declare: "some of our number to whom we gave no instruction have disturbed you" (EH). In the view of these scholars, Paul's account is accurate, but Luke has rewritten the account in order to suggest early agreement between Paul and the key apostles. This is not the only possible reading of Acts alongside Galatians, however. It should be remembered that the tone of biblical Greek is not signaled by "scare quotes" or by italics, and that it is very possible that Paul is being sarcastic when he uses the phrase "from James"; further, we don't know the chronology, and it may be that Paul has no information at the time that he wrote Galatians that James was not in agreement. At any rate, in this very letter, where he describes the face-off that he had with the wavering Peter concerning table fellowship with gentile Christians (Gal. 2:11–14ff.), Paul also describes staying with Peter for fifteen days; meeting James, the brother of the Lord; and deliberately visiting Jerusalem to make sure that his gospel work had not been done "in vain." Though he realizes that apostles (in this case, Peter) were capable of personal failure, he cares about the consonance of his message with theirs and checks out the content of his gospel against their witness. For him, no less than those disturbing the churches, the principle of apostolic authority held—even though he had directly met Jesus on the road to Damascus.

So, then, Galatians is not a letter about the difference between a faith governed by "ancestral traditions" (Gal. 1:14, cf. NRSV) over against *no* tradition, but about discerning the difference between living and dead tradition. As he declares at the end of this letter, "Peace be upon all who follow *this rule*" (Gal. 6:16 EH)—a way of faith that centers upon Jesus and the cross, that is witnessed to by the apostles together, even to the point of their bearing upon their bodies the stigmata of Christ (Gal. 6:17). This is a communal tradition passed on to persons by Paul in his person, by his oral word, by the common life he shares with the Church, by his writings (in LARGE LETTERS, Gal. 6:11), and in his body. It is a tradition about the Triune God—Father, Son, and Holy Spirit—at work in the Church.

All this is confirmed as we see Paul tackling other issues in the churches. Typically, he sends letters not in his own name only but in concert with others, like Timothy and Titus. This is his modus operandi in the letter known as 2 Thessalonians, where the congregation has been shaken by false reports of Paul's teaching that the Day of the Lord had come and gone and they had missed it. He repeats for them what he had verbally taught them earlier concerning the coming of Jesus. Much of this sounds like a paraphrase of Jesus' words concerning God's enemies, trials, and hope in the Synoptic Gospels (2 Thess. 2:3–10; cf. Mark 13:14, 22, 24–26 and parallels). Probably an early apostolic tradition of Jesus' teaching was repeated independently by Paul and by the Gospel writers. And so he urges his congregation: "Stand firm and hold to the *traditions* which you were taught, whether by word or by letter from us" (2:15 EH). The plural word "us" may be simply the "royal we," but it is far more likely that Paul is invoking the apostolic "we"—the "we" of those whom Jesus left as witnesses to his word.

Once he has established this, St. Paul goes on to tackle the problem of the brother who has adopted the lifestyle (3:6) described in the "VeggieTales" musical video *The Pirates Who Don't Do Anything*: "We are the pirates who don't do anything; we just stay at home and lie around." About his behavior, Paul declares that this is *not* illustrative of "the tradition" that the community had received through Paul and others—a large tradition that encompasses a way of life as well as teachings of faith and hope. These teachings did not *originate* with Paul or the other leaders, but they have it among them from the Lord and pass it on in the churches. Paul uses the word *para* in talking about the tradition that has come *alongside* the believers and which they have received (*par' hēmōn*, 3:6). Past history, how Christians should walk and believe in the present, and the hopeful goal toward which they are going are all encompassed in that Holy Tradition.

Paul follows a similar course as he handles other important and disputed matters in the various churches. In both 1 Corinthians 11 and 14 he deals with disruptions in worship that had sprung from the newfound freedom of women in the new covenant community. Here Paul resorts to several parts of the Tradition. First, he returns to the primeval Genesis account, speaking about woman as created to be the "glory" of man. He has, unfortunately, been misread by many on this score, including the great English poet John Milton, who in *Paradise Lost* restates this passage so as to establish a graded scale of being, suggesting that woman is made in the image of man, who is made in the image of Christ, who is the image of the Father.

This is not what St. Paul says here, however, for he never suggests that women are not also reflective of Christ's image—after all, these are instructions about how they should dress while praying and prophesying! However, women are also expressive of the glory of humanity and for that reason should not be the center of focus in a worship service: worship is for glorifying God, not for the exaltation of people. Paul goes on in his argument. He appeals to a more esoteric part of the tradition about cosmic worship, in the little phrase, "because of the angels" (1 Cor. 11:10). Recall that in Isaiah 6 the angels cover their feet and sing the Thrice-Holy Hymn, while in Revelation 4–5 they actually serve as *leaders* of the celestial worship, cuing the various parts of creation to adore the Lord in their peculiar way.[5] If God the Son acknowledges a head, and the glorious seraphim cover themselves as they fly, then why should women neglect to cover their heads, acknowledging the diversity of creation? In worship, men and women are to speak, it seems, antiphonally to each other: one group declares to the congregation the creaturely submission that is meet and right before utter Holiness; the other proclaims the hope of those who will be revealed as "*sons of God*" (anointed like Jesus, whether men or women) and who even now possess "the glorious freedom of God's children" (Rom. 8:19, 21 EH).

We must read this difficult section, and also chapter 14's instruction regarding silent submission among women, in such a way that we do not neutralize what Paul actually says—women *do* pray and prophesy in the assembly and they should comport themselves in humility when they do so. A particular type of silence is in view—refraining from unseemly debate, disruptive chattering, or an exhibition that calls attention to human willfulness or beauty.[6] Finally, the apostle

---

5. An implicit reminder of the angelic role in directing worship is consonant with the apostle's final word on worship to the congregation, that all things should be done with an eye to *taxis*, that is, "according to order" (1 Cor. 14:40 EH).

6. Several good exegetes have argued that 1 Cor. 14:33b–36 are not original to Paul. They have influenced, for example, the editors of the NRSV, who placed this section

appeals to nature (what it implies about the difference in the sexes) and to custom: "If anyone is inclined to be contentious, we have no such practice, nor do the churches of God" (11:16 ESV). This final appeal to the universal custom of the churches is similar to his closing exclamation in this argument: "What, did the word of God originate with *you*? Are *you* the only ones that it has reached?" (14:36 EH).

Whether he is arguing from common custom (in the case of head coverings) or from the actual Word of God, he is concerned about the arrogance of those who believe that it is their prerogative unilaterally to strike down common practices. Common customs may, perhaps, be changed—but in the churches even such human customs shouldn't be considered arbitrary, for they are based upon a common life and teaching that springs from the Holy Spirit. Not to despise the ways of our older siblings in the Church, and to discern what endures for our time over against what may change, requires humility, charity, and wisdom—that is to say, the mind of Christ, who "did not please himself" (Rom. 15:3). In a later chapter we will consider the matter of traditions that do not last as part of the Holy Tradition, how the Church has discerned this, and how we might follow the same pattern so as not to make mistakes in this area that could sap the energy or disrupt the unity of Christ's body.

The same problem of willful individualism was also marring the practice of the Lord's Supper in Corinth. The lack of concern for the whole body of Christ and the casual reception of this meal without self-examination are castigated by the apostle, who in 1 Corinthians 11 also tells them that meeting together in this way is *weakening* them rather than strengthening them as the Church. The remedy that he provides is clear: he refers them back to the tradition that he had received (11:27), reminding them that the Lord Jesus was betrayed and gave himself—so how can they belittle each other? And should

---

in parentheses as though it were an aside and not part of Paul's flow of argument. However, the verses are found in every ancient manuscript and have been read as authentic throughout the centuries. It would seem that the judgment to excise them only provides a "solution" in the case of readers who attribute authority exclusively to original manuscripts as reproduced by scholars and as though God does not continue to lead the Church. I do not think that we can find an easy solution by removing the offending verses—and, indeed, what will we do with 1 Tim. 2:11 and 1 Pet. 3:1, which also associate women with silence?

they not give themselves to each other, just as they give themselves to God in worship? The purpose of the Supper is not to eat and so individually satisfy oneself, but to participate in Christ, to proclaim the Lord's death, and to anticipate his return—all this to build up the Church. They are to receive with thanks the gifts given by Holy Tradition, to guard the Supper's significance, and to proclaim that life to others. As he says earlier: "The cup that we bless, is it not the communion of the blood of Christ? The bread which we break, is it not the communion of the body of Christ? For we, though many, are one bread, one body: for we are all partakers of that one bread" (1 Cor. 10:16–17 EH).

So What?

We should take heart that in the very place where St. Paul details the unity of the Church, he was aware of the problem of discord and threatening schism. Being part of a tradition that brings together many in true unity is not an easy thing. Indeed, in Romans 11, the action of God the Holy Spirit in engrafting the gentiles into the body was seen as something that is, from one perspective, "contrary to nature." Gentiles did not have, after all, the *proto-evangelion* (pre-gospel teaching) of the Law and Prophets to guide them, and much of the preparation that God had given to the Jewish people was foreign to them culturally. To the Greeks, for example, circumcision was a disfigurement of the body, and the faithfulness of one man to one wife an indication of invirility. Likewise, for the Romans "humility" was no virtue at all, and not to expose a frail newborn or unwanted girl on the hillside was sheer sentimentality. We face similar problems today, of course, though the debates are framed in a different vein. Today the Church is finding herself embattled because there are perceived conflicts between the Scriptures, the ongoing life (or Tradition) of the Church, cultural norms, the present leading of the Spirit, and the teaching of leaders. Moreover, the arenas of discord remain very similar, for example, as classical Christianity[7] challenges cultural norms on sexuality, while

7. I prefer to use the descriptor "classical" rather than "conservative," since one of the hallmarks of Christianity, as passed down from its inception, is that it has both

revisioning Christians assume that this is one of those traditions that must be modified for the vitality (or relevance) of the Church. In this decade we hear pronouncements such as that made by Linda M. Maloney, a priest in the Anglican Church of Canada:

> It is not good practice to try to make Paul hold only those opinions we ourselves think acceptable. [*So far, so good,* I responded, on reading this. But she goes on . . .] So in matters of gender relations and sexuality: Paul may have thought differently from me, and he's entitled to his opinion, but I'm also entitled to mine. To me, that doesn't represent rejecting the authority of Scripture, but honoring it. Paul wrote in his context; I read in mine; the Holy Spirit is with us in the writing and in the reading.[8]

This astonishing statement is hermeneutically honest because it chastises the practices of some interpreters who are (mis)shaping translations and reading the Bible against its grain because of their contemporary agenda. But then she makes a disturbing move: when my opinion collides with "the opinion" of a scriptural author, that is not a problem to be wrestled with. Instead, the Holy Spirit can be appealed to as we read.

Our new context is the trump card, the deciding factor. Her statement is similar to those that we are now hearing in pro-choice circles: "Yes, the embryo and fetus are forms of a human being, but they are not legal persons until so recognized by law, and it is our decision concerning whether they should be nurtured and brought into human society." I am not quite sure which type of revisionist is harder to debate—the one who allows Scripture and reality to stay intact but who willfully makes choices against them or the one who tries to modify Scripture and reality in order to justify contrary actions. (Examples of the latter would be: "Paul didn't *mean* to critique homosexuality *per se*" or "This unborn bit of tissue isn't really a baby.")

In the light of these different contemporary approaches to interpretation, we can see that the models of decision making that we

---

a conserving and a renovating principle. By "classical" I mean a Christianity that is committed to Scriptures, to the Church, and to the Great Tradition.

8. This statement was made in a discussion group for Anglicans and distributed to members of the "Canang-List" on June 27, 2003. For information on the group, see http://canang.ca/. Accessed January 2012.

have traced in Scripture (particularly in Acts and the Pauline Epistles) will serve the Church well in making its contemporary decisions. We have, as part of the lively treasure transmitted to us, principles and practices delivered to us by which we too can learn to make godly decisions that neither reject nor reenvision the Scriptures, but that recognize its lively word to us in the twenty-first century. To this we will turn in chapter 6. However, before moving on to the nitty-gritty of discerning the difference between enduring Holy Tradition and human traditions with more limited value, we still have more to learn about the nature of Tradition—first, how it is practiced and received by the whole Church together, with a dynamic that is more complex than that of top-down authoritarianism (chapter 4); second, how Tradition demonstrates the utterly personal nature of our life in Christ, and that it borrows this characteristic from our personal God, who delights to make persons of us all (chapter 5).

– 4 –

The Blessed Delivery

Receiving in Both Directions

For who has known the mind of the Lord, or who has been his counselor? Or who has first given to Him that it might be paid back to the human giver? For from Him and through Him and to Him are all things. To Him be the glory forever! (Rom. 11:34–36 EH)

Luke's Gospel has a notable central episode (10:1–24) that is not found—at least intact—in any of the other Gospels. It is that missionary sequence in which the Lord commissions seventy of his disciples to go ahead of him, preparing the way, like mini–John the Baptists, in the places where their master himself will arrive. In sending them out, as lambs among wolves, and vulnerable like himself, Jesus declares, "The one who hears you hears me, and the one who rejects you rejects me, and the one who rejects me rejects Him who sent me" (Luke 10:16 EH).

A Chain of Command?

Jesus' words startle us in our twenty-first-century egalitarian age with what looks to be a chain of command—from the Almighty One, to

Jesus, to the Twelve (whom he has appointed in the previous chapter) with the seventy, to us. When we read this Scripture as applying beyond its historical context, we realize that "the one who hears" the apostle is me or you; or, in a darker mode, it is we who might reject them and their teaching. Historically, of course, we are among those who have heard *others*, who heard others, who heard others, who heard the seventy and the apostles, who heard Jesus. For twenty long centuries there has been a God-directed delivery system, so to speak, so that the word of Jesus still is proclaimed vitally and with dynamic effect throughout the world.

Yet Jesus' words may seem troubling to us. Perhaps they are not quite so troubling as his (to us) appalling statement to the Canaanite woman who was begging his help, "It is not right to give the children's bread to the (little) dogs!" (Matt. 15:26 EH). Like those upsetting words, Jesus' words here to the seventy imply that there is an order in the way that God deals with the world. With the Canaanite woman, Jesus was acknowledging (albeit in a manner foreign to our sensibilities) that God was following an order in history: to the Jew first (and then to the gentile). With Luke 10:16, Jesus actually speaks about authority structures and about how those who will reject his disciples are really rejecting him, the head of the seventy. There are other similar statements of solidarity in the Gospels, such as when Jesus said that those of the nations who gave a cup of water in his name to his followers were doing it, really, for him (Matt. 25:40). Somehow we don't mind that upbeat assurance quite so much. But how can it be that he indicated this kind of identified authority as the possession of those seventy who were speaking in his name? Was he setting up an unbreakable hierarchy, and to what end? Is it unequivocally true that "the one who rejects you rejects me"?

After all, the world can hardly be blamed for dismissing the words of weak and fallible human beings who may or may not accurately represent Jesus, either in word or in deed. On top of that, ordinary humans hardly possess the life, the glory, or the stature of that One true Human Being who is also God. Frequently, and with reason, we lament the weakness of the Church and speak with compassion about those who *think* that they have rejected Christianity, when all along they have been offended by God's people and so received a compromised version of the Way. Thus we come up against one of the major problems we have in acknowledging the value of tradition—we assume that tradition is simply the *human* guarding of what may have been a divine revelation, and we know that humans can be mistaken about what they have seen and heard. The idea of tradition confers some sort of authority upon the one passing on the tradition; we are skeptical in this day and age of authority structures, especially when that involves leaders in history whom we can neither control nor interrogate.

Jesus, though innocent, was never naive. He too "knew what was in the human being" (John 2:25 EH). Despite all this, Jesus says to the seventy that the one who hears *them* is actually hearing *him*: then he sends them out with authority to preach, to heal, and to cast out demons. We should, of course, pause to notice that in this story he is sending out a whole bevy of ambassadors (unnamed here, but listed with variation in ancient works other than the New Testament). His commission and his conferred authority reach more broadly here than the vision vouchsafed to the three key apostles who saw his Transfiguration or to the twelve who were intimate with him throughout the time of his ministry. Yet the words appear to be specifically directed to those whom he is commissioning rather than to all believers. Jesus assumes a radical solidarity between himself and those who have been in his presence, whom he is sending out to prepare the way. (I have no doubt that the words may well be applied to missionaries whom the Holy Spirit, with the Church, is sending out today; however, it is important for us, in the first place, to see the particularity of this mission and to feel the full weight of Jesus' selection of *some* to do a particular thing.)

How remarkable! Despite the tendency of human failure, *persons* are commissioned to communicate the *person* Jesus, who communicates God the Father—our faith is, from beginning to end, personal. It is not simply a body of teaching material that can be deposited without remainder in a book; it is not a series of practices that can be learned in a detached fashion from a manual for living or a "how to" book; it is not a philosophy or an ethic that presents itself to the thinker as an object of study or of critique. If a humanly received, guarded, and transmitted tradition is part and parcel of the gospel, then we need to look carefully at how this dynamic works. Already in the last chapter we observed the various checks and balances that accompany the making of decisions in the early Church: Peter is commanded to go, Cornelius is informed that he will come, the angel has gone in before, Peter appeals to the Law and Prophets as he proclaims Jesus, Peter is interrogated by some of his colleagues and must answer to the apostles and elders in Jerusalem, there is somewhat of a resolution but then the debate is ongoing, Barnabas and Saul give their two cents, Peter speaks again to the council, James recalls all that the Lord has told and shown them, and the entire council together prays and acts, reaching out to the gentile Christians. No one person has total authority, though there are clearly key players, some with key bits of knowledge, some with particular authority. Yet even one of those with authority (Peter) can be corrected by another (Paul) when he is mistaken (cf. Gal. 2).

All these brothers (and sisters) listening together and hearing what God has said, and is saying, come to be strengthened in the faith, for God has come to be with them in Jesus, who became flesh, and God has come to be near them by the Spirit, who dwells among them. The wonder of our faith is this: the Father is life, love, and light in himself, needing nothing, and yet he reaches out to us by the Son through the Holy Spirit. As Jesus remarks after the seventy come home in triumph, "All things have been delivered to me by my Father; and no one knows who the Son is except the Father, or who the Father is except the Son and any one to whom the Son chooses to reveal him" (Luke 10:22). This intercommunion between Father and Son (and Spirit) is mirrored in the Church, where each person has a role and yet where there is clearly authority for leadership located in the Twelve and the seventy. In this chapter, then, we will troubleshoot regarding the specific problem that we possess in our day—our suspicion about those in authority and our fear of abuse of authority. I believe that of particular help to us will be a curious paradox found in two different words proclaimed by Jesus concerning reception of tradition and gifts in the Church. This paradox will help us to appreciate how the Church becomes a matrix for the living interactions between God's people as they receive and are received. Authority and recognition are exercised not only from the top down but also are located in unexpected places in the Church; at the same time, the Holy Spirit has given leaders as a particular gift to the Church (cf. Eph. 4:11).

God the Giver

As we think about tradition, its transmission and reception, this passage of Luke's Gospel demonstrates in living color why tradition is so important: it shows the vibrant nature of what Jesus passed on or delivered to his followers. Jesus prepares the seventy for ministry by telling them that they will be offering to others what they have received. On top of this he emphasizes that the original Actor, the first Giver of this gift that they will deliver, is God himself. The Gospel and their preaching are part of a grand and holy transaction enacted by an almighty and holy God.

In the first epistle of Peter, we hear the same thing. The letter speaks with wonder about a blessed delivery, the "many-splendored grace" that the Church has received from God. The letter then goes on with this solemn instruction: "Let the one who speaks do it as one who utters [the very] oracles of God; whoever renders service, as one who renders it by the [very] strength that God supplies; in order that in everything God may be glorified through Jesus Christ" (1 Pet. 4:10–11 EH). And then the letter breaks into a doxology. God the giver gives, we receive, and we return the gift back to God by serving our brothers and sisters. He gives, and we become givers ourselves. The Giver changes us.

Perhaps those seventy were tempted, on hearing Jesus' words, to receive them as a carte blanche of authority or merely as a theological truth, something theoretical that puts God's stamp of approval on the message. They were about to learn, on the ground, that this commission was not for their own benefit, nor was it mere theory or correct doctrine. Rather, Jesus is drawing them into the modus operandi of God himself! God had entrusted to them a delivery blessed above all other things, a message concerning the gift of his own self to the world in Jesus. As they continued in mission, as they saw what would happen, these missionaries would come to understand more deeply what it meant to deliver God's gift. The delivery begins by entering into homes, healing the sick, and announcing the nearness of God. It may involve rejection and, eventually for some, the harsh enactment of it by their own martyrdom. (Stephen is on most of the traditional lists of the seventy.) By the time that their entire life's mission was accomplished, they would understand more fully the message that they bore (for Cleopas, also named as one of the seventy, would be further taught by Jesus, hearing about the grave necessity of Messiah's death, leading to the resurrection, cf. Luke 24:26–27). They would also understand more fully their own place within the community that Jesus had forged by the Holy Spirit, not as autocratic leaders, but as servants who were privileged to be with Jesus. Perhaps John the elder articulates this communal understanding best:

> That which was from the beginning, which we have heard, which we have seen with our eyes, which we have looked upon and touched with our hands, concerning the Word of life . . . that which we have seen and heard we proclaim . . . so that you may have fellowship with us; and our fellowship is with the Father and with his Son Jesus Christ. (1 John 1:1, 3)

What the seventy were sent to announce to the townspeople around them was the offer of fellowship with them, with the Word of Life and with the Father. God was the Giver, the One who authorized this astonishing delivery. And when God gives, things are never the same: as the Scriptures put it, his "word shall not return to him void" (Isa. 55:11 EH). In mission, in living, in the passing on of what they had received, the disciples would come more fully to understand Jesus' strange words about their names being on the heavenly roll: "Nevertheless do not rejoice in this, that the spirits are subject to you; but rejoice that your names are written in heaven" (Luke 10:20). They were handling holy things, and proclaiming the good news to those whom God was setting aside for himself, those who would be their brothers and sisters. The ability of the seventy to command the spirits (Luke 10:17) was indeed their humble part in the downfall of Satan, which Jesus saw and proclaimed as they returned in victory (Luke 10:18). Such powerful activity was not intended to bolster their sense of pride or position, but was instead a gift to the Church. The gift of themselves, in its fullness, could well involve their ultimate sacrifice in service if they followed in the steps of the great Servant-King.

God the Gift

Indeed, we see in this episode far more than a gift or commission given *by* God. Not only is God the giver but God is also the gift. Jesus, filled with the Spirit, declares to them, "Blessed are the eyes which see what you see! For I tell you that many prophets and kings desired to see what you see, and did not see it, and to hear what you hear, and did not hear it" (Luke 10:23–24). But what had their eyes seen? What mystery had they glimpsed, unseen by prophets and kings? Jesus himself! Jesus, in this exclamation of "blessed," is reflecting with joy upon that same truth proclaimed in awe in Hebrews 1:2—"in these last days, God has spoken through his Son" (EH). God does not give simply information, God does not give simply a new law, God does not bestow simply authority or simply grace, but God gives *himself*. Among us has been the God-Man Jesus; God gives himself personally to human persons, who in turn represent, as far as we are able, this holy God. To the seventy, Jesus remarked "the one who hears you hears me" (Luke 10:16 EH) and in saying this he also implied "the one who hears me hears the One who sent me." It is this thoroughly personal aspect that separates our Christian Way from all the other ways and -isms and philosophies of the world.

I am reminded of when I was a young mother with three children, habitually meeting another young mother on the playground near our home in an old neighborhood in Montreal. After some conversation, I discovered that she was a Jehovah's Witness. We agreed on many things, but not on the automatic or mechanical nature of the faith nor on the identity of Jesus. These things were connected, I think. To her, the faith was a series of morals and doctrines to pass on to her children: "good things in, good things out; junk in, junk out," she would say. For her, Jesus was, above all other descriptors, the Teacher. Of course, it is not that this was wrong. But she had missed the mystery of life and person-hood—she did not see Jesus as a Person who could be known and who was seeking us. Because of this, she also could not fully appreciate the mystery of her children's own personhood. They were more like pets to be trained than like tiny miniature images of God, with wills and hearts and minds that could be reached only by the Holy Spirit. The discipline of the Witnesses exhibits a rather brittle character and is indeed sometimes cruelly rigid. Trespassers are "disciplined" by very strict shunning and for long periods of time. The Witnesses are strong on judgment but not so knowledgeable about mercy and forgiveness. Indeed they do not understand judgment in all its fullness, for they do not recognize that God *himself* died in the flesh to exhaust the power of sin and death. My prayer is that when people encounter us, we are vibrant enough that, with all our faults, they can see through us to the living Christ. The longevity and popularity of the classical Christian name "Christo-pher" is a testimony to the Christian understanding of what it means to be a Christian: not simply one who follows a discipline of life (though we do this), not simply one who believes a certain creed (though this is important), but one whose whole life "bears" (the Greek is *pherō*) and so exhibits Christ, whose person is imprinted by this Person of persons. We bear, or carry, the living Tradition, the One who has been given to us. Moreover, when we see others, we are encouraged not to see simply them but something far greater. As St. Paul puts it, we ought not to see others "according to the flesh" but as they truly are (or will be) when perfected by the Holy Spirit: they, with us, are invited to live eternally as his children, ruling with him in all wisdom and love.

The Holy Spirit was surely at work like this in the hearts of the seventy as they went on the mission that Jesus had given them. As they went, they carried the name of Jesus like a banner, not just over them but in their hearts and imaginations. Otherwise the demons could not have been subdued nor the illnesses healed nor even the message believed. After all, they had *been with* him. Their eyes and ears and hearts were full of the healings, the stirring words, the humble triumph of this One whom they were proclaiming. And that name was powerful on their lips and in their hearts—"even the demons submit to us in your name," they marvel when they come back to their Master (Luke 10:17 EH). Jesus does not pour cold water on their enthusiasm, but he does redirect their eyes. It is as if he said to them, "You think *that* is wonderful? But I have seen the *great enemy* of God fall: his days are numbered! Indeed, because of me you do have authority. But there is something even more wonderful: it's not the position you have, it's not what you can *do*, it's who you are! You are members of God's family, your names have been written into the family register!" (cf. Luke 10:18–20). What is more important than the success of the seventy is that God has given them the very gift of himself. Jesus, the Son, is in their midst, giving himself for them, showing them the Father, and enabling them to pass this spiritual sight on to others.

This is the mystery long awaited not only by human beings, but "even angels longed to see it," we are told in 1 Peter 1:12 (EH). Here, in the flesh, is the Holy One. This is the mystery of the ages. As they have received this One, they are blessed! And so are we, because we too have received, from others who learned, ultimately, through them. Consider the encouragement of this nineteenth-century hymn that we should revel in this mystery:

> Name Him, brothers, name Him,
> With love as strong as death,
> But with awe and wonder,
> And with bated breath;
> He is GOD the Saviour,
> He is CHRIST the LORD,
> Ever to be worshipped,
> Trusted and adored.[1]

Of course, the eyes of the disciples were at this time only partially opened. More and more they would marvel at the generosity of the divine Giver and grow in astonishment concerning the strange beauty of the One who was the Gift of gifts, the "inexpressible gift" (2 Cor. 9:15). They still had the last supper to attend, the agony and trial to observe, the cross upon which to gaze. And they still awaited the revelation of the risen Jesus, who would come to them with teaching and feed them. More than that, he would come with his remarkable presence, causing their hearts to burn and their eyes to grasp even more. Like their master, they too would come to know the fullness of God's second great Gift—yet the gift is One!—the Holy Spirit. As the second-century leader of the Church St. Irenaeus would put it, the Son and the Holy Spirit are the two hands of the Father,[2] reaching out to embrace us. As the Church grew, they would be led together into even more knowledge, as Jesus promised in John 16:12–13, each new Christian reflecting more and more of the glory that had come among them (2 Cor. 3:17–18). This One is the *only* Gift that "keeps on giving," the only Tradition that endures forever, despite what popular advertisements might claim!

1. This hymn is in the public domain; the lyrics were written by Caroline Noel in 1870.
2. St. Irenaeus, *Against Heresies* 4, preface.

The strangeness of the Giver and of the Gift is indicated in the unexpected path that Jesus traced and also in the path that he sets out before his followers. Because we are prone to self-centeredness, error, and sin, Scripture often gives a corrective for us. We began with what looked to be a chain of authority, from the Father to the Son to the apostles (the twelve and the seventy) to those who would become the rest of the Church. Yet, just before being sent out on this mission, the seventy were given a strange word to prevent them from glorifying the role that they had been given, as though it were the main thing. We need to move *back* in the Gospel narrative and recall that, before they had the opportunity to heal and to displace demons, Jesus had placed a child in their midst. Jesus' words to them at that time also involved the idea of reception: "The one who receives this child in my name receives me: and the one who receives me receives him who sent me: for the one who is least among you all is the one who is indeed great" (Luke 9:48 EH). Here, then, is the same language we have met in the commissioning passage ("the one who . . . me . . . him who sent me")—but the direction of the "chain" is quite different.

God in Us and among Us

It looks as though we need to add a further mystery to the two marvels that we have collected (*God is the Giver*; *God is the Gift*). In this striking object lesson, Jesus impresses upon our imaginations something else: *God is in and among us, the recipients.* And just who is the recipient here? Is it the child? Or is it the apostles? Jesus puts the spotlight upon the little one in their midst. Whenever the leaders whom Jesus has appointed receive this child, they are receiving Jesus, he says; and therefore they are receiving the Father. His words are, indeed, a preview of the great prayer of thanksgiving that he will utter when the seventy return: Jesus thanks the Father "that he has hidden these things from the wise, and revealed them to babies" (Matt. 11:25 EH). The apostles, no less than this child, are infants in Christ. The least is, in God's economy, the greatest. It looks, then, as though there is a chain of *receiving* as well as a chain of *giving*. Not only are the seventy to act in the name of Jesus when they speak, heal, wield

God-given authority, and give out the living tradition; they also act in the name of Jesus when they lovingly receive the one who seems insignificant. In *that* person they must see the very image of God, the one for whom God yearns, the one for whom the Gift was designed. Moreover, they themselves are children of God. So then, the humblest child is himself or herself a gift to the apostles—hidden beneath that unassuming infant face is God's own beauty and grace, the potential for God's strength to be "made perfect in weakness" (2 Cor. 12:9).

Here is the potent answer to our discomfort over the chain of command, our worry that God has set up an oppressive hierarchy—God works not just top down but also bottom up. There is not only a chain of command but a chain of reception and of bottom-up giving. Deep answers to deep. It is tempting simply to take the easy road and allow these two words of Jesus to cancel each other out: If both the apostles and the child are gifts, then they are exactly the same, are they not? Well, yes and no. As with most paradoxes, the truth emerges as we hear both seemingly contradictory words together rather than letting them bleed into each other or neutralize each other. We need to hear them both in all their fullness and with the challenge that they issue to our imaginations:

> The one who hears you hears me, and the one who rejects you rejects me, and the one who rejects me rejects Him who sent me. (Luke 10:16 EH)

> The one who receives this child in my name receives me, and the one who receives me receives Him who sent me, for the one who is least among you all is the one who is indeed great. (Luke 9:48 EH)

It is not the case that the apostles and the child have the same position and the same role. Yet both apostle and child have received from God (they are children to him) and both the apostle and the child will receive something from the gift of each other—not the identical gift, but each a valuable gift. There is indeed an order that Jesus established for the churches, since he chose the Twelve with prayer and commissioned the seventy with words of authority. (And we are told in the Acts that these leaders appointed others in the churches, as did Paul.) It is ultimately from these twelve and these seventy that the gospel was bequeathed to others all over the world, and ultimately all faithful pastors today have received from those who taught them, going back to the apostles themselves. Much of what they have learned comes through the Holy Scriptures, but of course these books are themselves the library of the Church, compiled and handed on to us. Other things they have learned—the way of living, praying, trusting, sacrificing—not from sacred books but in the flesh from those who lived with them in the flesh. It is not simply St. Paul who has said, with reason, to his "children" "Imitate us!" (cf. 2 Thess. 3:7, 9) and "have this mind among yourselves that was also in Christ Jesus" (Phil. 2:5 EH).

It is a fantasy of reverse snobbery to declare that we are all "equal" in Christ and therefore we need to pay attention to no one else for guidance. After all, even St. Paul, the privileged recipient of an astounding vision, was compelled to submit himself, first to Ananias in Damascus and then to the apostles in Jerusalem. Democracy is an excellent form of government in a fallen world, with various checks and balances so that the law applies to everyone—but democracy cannot make everyone equally wise, or gifted, or even sacrificial. We do not know how things will be when God is all in all, when we are perfected in Christ, but I suspect that the faithful will always be grateful, and show deference, to those who guided them in the faith. We have received, and so we owe a debt of gratitude and respect.

So, then, there is a natural and right direction of reception from, can we say, the "top down," which we must surely acknowledge and which we will not despise. But the direction of action and reception goes the other direction as well. Even those whose role it is to teach and to lead are recipients, and sometimes they receive from the strangest places. The story is told of a tiny Orthodox parish in Alaska among whom the new bishop came for his first visit. The bishop celebrated the liturgy with them and gave the homily. Then he told the priest of the parish that he would be happy to entertain questions if the people would care to ask some. The people began to ask very basic questions: "Who is Jesus? Whose Son is he? What does the Holy Spirit do? Who is he?" After a while, the bemused bishop turned to the priest and said quietly, "I don't mean any disrespect, father. But it seems to me that your people are not very well acquainted with Orthodoxy." Without missing a beat the priest responded, "Oh, no, your Grace! They are very well acquainted with Orthodoxy. But they want to know if you are, because if you are not, you cannot be their bishop!"

I have no idea why these people felt it necessary to test their bishop in this manner: perhaps there is more to the story than just this one scene. However, I do know that even in a Church that takes authority very seriously—in Orthodoxy the bishop is understood to be consecrated with an authority going back to the apostles—the priest's rejoinder was appropriate, if bold. For the bishop—and the priest too—receive *from the people* an active assent—the declaration "Axios!" ("He is worthy!") at the consecration or ordination and the "Amen!" at every liturgy. It can never "seem right" simply to one leader (claiming the Holy Spirit's inspiration); it must always "seem right to the Holy Spirit and to *us*." There is, then, a real authority among those who seem to be weak, for they are, says Jesus, the greatest in the kingdom. The one who prays must hear an answering "Amen!" or there is no community at prayer. When a leader receives someone into the Church, this is a gift to the whole Church, not simply a grace to the one who is received. Among the people there are those with prophetic gifts who are not part of the formal leadership but whom the Holy Spirit uses, from time to time, to keep on course those who teach and lead. And there are those with practical gifts without which those who teach and administer could never fulfill their calling. Perhaps in this day of individualism we need to hear again about the importance of leadership and be called to respect formal authorities in the Church, both past and present. But we need never fear, with the way that God works, that the Church will devolve into a mere institution, a business, an oppressive machine with a CEO instead of a pastor, or an oligarchy, ruling for the sake of its own prestige. For God works not only in the normal channels of authority but in unexpected ways too: for every prince and priest there is also a prophet or prophetess!

Strategies "From Above" and "From Below"

We might have expected this strange dynamic had we looked more carefully at the modus operandi of God in his divine and ineffable mission to the world. We can think of his rescue and transformation of us both in terms of a mission from above and an infiltration from below. So, for example, many have pictured Jesus as the hero who came to "bind the strong man" (Mark 3:27; Matt. 12:29; Luke 11:21–22) so that we could be rescued. Similarly, he gives to us the ultimate example of God's love, displaying it for all on the cross, so that we might ourselves come to know what love is. Or, he is our sacrifice, the one who stands in for us, and has the position to counter our sin with his righteousness. These ways of understanding salvation picture an attack on evil and a mission of rescue from above. Jesus, in the words of St. Paul, is the "man of heaven," come to undo the error of "the man of dust" (1 Cor. 15:48); he is, in the words of the evangelist, the One "from above" who prevails over the blindness of those who are "below" (John 8:23). "He has delivered us from the dominion of darkness and transferred us to the kingdom of his beloved Son" (Col. 1:13). A victorious Messiah has accomplished God's mission!

At the same time, we hear in the New Testament of the interior and immanent work of the Holy Spirit. Romans 8:22–27 speaks of the Holy Spirit as dwelling and acting powerfully within the inner shrine of the world, the Church: the fallen world longs for redemption, human beings within that world cry out, the Church intercedes for the pain of the world, and the Holy Spirit (among the faithful) intercedes when their cries are inarticulate or uninformed. As St. Paul puts it, "The One who searches the hearts of humans knows what is the mind of the Spirit, because the Spirit intercedes for the saints according to the will of God" (Rom. 8:27 EH). Matching God's penetration, or attack, or rescue venture from the outside into our world is the immanent, interior, wooing, transforming work of the Holy Spirit: God works from inside as well as from outside.

Nor is it helpful to rigidly assign the "outside" work to the advent of God the Son and the "inside" work to the Holy Spirit given at Pentecost. After all, we are told that the Holy Spirit hovered upon the virgin Mary, causing her to become the "Theotokos," or "God-bearer." Some of the early Church fathers speak about the Holy Spirit as resting upon the Son—the picture that we certainly get from the descent of the dove at his baptism. In a sense, then, the Holy Spirit comes from "outside" as well. Similarly, to speak about the Incarnation in terms of the visitation to our world by an exterior God the Son is not accurate. It is not as though Jesus were whisked here on a supernatural Star Trek vessel and beamed down, only to be beamed up again when the mission was accomplished. No, a deeper and more satisfying way of understanding this miracle is to use the patristic language—"God assumed humanity," taking it completely to himself. Jesus plunged himself into our world, even to the point of taking on our death and sin, and so exhausted their power. A mere visit would not do! As St. Gregory of Nazianzen put it, "What is not assumed is not healed."[3] Even more than this, the assumption, or taking up of our humanity unto God in the God-Man Jesus, has consequences that go far beyond our redemption. God's design seems always to have been this kind of deep communion with us (he "walked with Adam in the garden"), and the New Testament makes it clear that God intends, by this astonishing move, to do something far more radical than accomplish our rescue. God indeed desires to make known to us "the riches of the glory of this mystery, which is Christ in [us], the hope of glory" (Col. 1:27). So then, the Incarnation itself is deeply interior to humanity and not merely a temporary drawing near, since by his Ascension Jesus demonstrates that our nature (even our flesh!) has been eternally joined to him.

God's strategy, then, is two-pronged and so matches both his awe-inspiring transcendence and his startling immanence in our world. If God works both from above and from below, then it is not surprising that in the Church these two dynamics are also at work. We do not need to dispute God's transcendent power in order to embrace his closeness to us. We do not need to question God's immanence in order to safeguard his dignity. Christians are neither Deists, who posit a God totally separate from the world, nor pantheists, who confuse the Creator with the creation: we have the best of both worlds.

Order and Mutuality in Tradition

And so it is with the living Tradition of the Church. It exists in our common life at all levels and moves in both directions, (so-called) "top

3. St. Gregory of Nazianzen, epistle 101, "To Cledonius the Priest Against Apollinarius," in Philip Schaff and Henry Wace, *Nicene and Post-Nicene Fathers of the Christian Church*, vol. 7, *Cyril of Jerusalem, Gregory Nazianzen* (Grand Rapids: Eerdmans, 1955), 439–42.

down" and (so-called) "bottom up." We have no need to downplay
the significance of the apostles, nor of our contemporary pastors, in
order to safeguard the importance of every Christian. Nor do those
who lead need to guard their own position and act in a manner that
runs roughshod over those in their care. There is both an order and
a mutuality to be viewed with awe in the Triune Godhead and to be
lived out in the Church with care, love, and prayer.

Earlier generations had some difficulty understanding the aspect
of mutuality that is so key to the faith—it was some time before
Christians heeded the intimations in Scripture with regard to slavery,
for example, and acted upon these, even though there is a specific
letter (Philemon) that commends a believing slave to his master as a
"brother." Today, it is clear that the opposite is the case. Egalitari-
anism and democracy are so central to our way of thinking, as is a
mind-set intent upon "rights," that we often think it beneath our
dignity, and even unchristian, to give honor to those who lead the
Church. How quickly comes to our mind Jesus' warning, "Call no
man father," but how reluctantly we remember these words: "Let
the presbyters who rule well be counted worthy of double honor,
especially those who labor in (proclaiming) the word and (teaching)
doctrine" (1 Tim. 5:17 EH). The very pattern of God's Triune life,
and how he has worked with us in history, should lead us to expect
that the living Tradition of the Church will be a matter of teaching
and reception, respect and recognition, permeating all places and
all positions in the Church. We do not need to flatten out the family
onto an artificial "equal plane" in order to recognize the worth of
every member. Nor should any one leader have an exaggerated sense
of importance but should instead cultivate the mind of Christ, as in
Philippians 2:5–11.

A quick consideration of how Paul upheld "hierarchy" (literally,
"holy headship"), while also recognizing mutuality, is very instructive.
He sees husband and wife in a particular relationship, even while he
recognizes their mutual interdependence. In reflecting upon the gospel
and holy history, he acknowledges, in the transmission of the tradition, the primacy of Israel "to whom was the adoption, and the glory,
and the covenants, and the giving of the law, and the worship, and
the promises, and whose are the fathers, and from whom . . . came

the Messiah" (Rom. 9:4–5 EH). He then goes on to recognize that believing gentiles are now mysteriously leading the way, illuminating it for Jews who have ignored Jesus (Rom. 11:25). The mutuality does not destroy the hierarchy, nor the hierarchy the mutuality: they stand together, paradoxically but fruitfully.

As we return to Luke 10, with which we started—Jesus' commission and debriefing of the seventy—we hear him also acknowledge God's ability to turn things on their head, even while the head is not destroyed. He speaks, in the debriefing section, of kings and prophets, those honored siblings of the past, who are now surpassed by the seventy, some of them unlearned men. He has, in his commissioning, established seventy elders in the Church. Yet he reminds us that all of this comes from God, and that, indeed, they are not wise in their own right (for they are really "lambs," 10:3, and "babes," 10:21). To these fledgling leaders, he declares in joy: "Blessed are the eyes that see what you see" (10:23). His words were historical, establishing the unique place of the apostles and the seventy in the beginnings of the Church. But his words concern not only them but us as well, since through their witness we have come to see too. His words come to us through the evangelist Luke, who heard this story from the apostles or, perhaps, was among the seventy. We are dependent upon them, but, by the Holy Spirit, we too see with the eye of faith the Wonder of wonders—God incarnate. We *personally* come to know that One who was delivered over into human hands but wields his authority from a cross. This One calls us both to receive him and his teaching, through the lips of others, and to receive others in his name, or to recognize as brothers and sisters those whom our pastors receive in his name, giving the "Amen."[4] He calls us to do this together, as his body.

He is the Giver.

He is the Gift.

He is (by the Holy Spirit) indwelling us, the Recipients,
    both personally and as a Church.

---

4. In the Orthodox tradition, as a new member of the Church is baptized and/or received in the rite of Chrismation (anointing with holy oil), the celebrant imposes the oil while the entire congregation declares, in agreement, "Sealed!" This is an action of reception by the entire Church.

In God's economy, we are both dependent upon others yet con-nected directly to him—the Word is delivered to us and also has its direct blessed effect upon us, so that we bring blessing to the Church into which he engrafts us. We are, by his action and presence in his-tory, recipients of a blessed delivery. And we are, by his action and presence, and by the action and presence of our siblings in Christ, among those whom he called "blessed." The answer to our misgivings about oppressive hierarchy may not be what we expected, but it is bracing and corrective. Here we are, at the long end of transmission, dependent upon the apostles but also upon numerous others for our understanding of the faith. Half of our New Testament came from the pen of one who was an educated rabbi but who called himself "the least of the saints" because he had persecuted the Church. Most of us are gentiles, dependent upon a Jewish Messiah who was also the true Adam. Half of us are women, created subsequent to Adam—but from our kind was born the One who has turned the world upside down. The proclamation of God's Word and the handing down of our family ways are matters that call not for shrill voices demand-ing equal rights but for faithfulness and humility, as God calls on us to exercise these within the company of the Church. May Jesus' words about the seventy and about the little child help us to grapple with this strange state of affairs—a reality that we could never have conceived, combining headship or order with authentic mutuality, composed of frail people with diverse callings. With this in mind, let us turn to look at the wholly *personal* aspect of Tradition, as seen in the Scriptures. "Who has known the mind of the Lord? . . . For from him and through him and to him are all things" (Rom. 11:34, 36).

– 5 –

TRADITION AS GOD'S
PERSONAL GIFT

I will extol thee, my God, O king; and I will bless thy name for ever
and ever. Every day will I bless thee; and I will praise thy name for
ever and ever. Great *is* the LORD, and greatly to be praised; and his
greatness *is* unsearchable. One generation shall praise thy works to
another, and shall declare thy mighty acts. I will speak of the glorious
honour of thy majesty, and of thy wondrous works. . . . The LORD *is*
gracious, and full of compassion; slow to anger, and of great mercy. The
LORD *is* good to all: and his tender mercies *are* over all his works. All
thy works shall praise thee, O LORD; and thy saints shall bless thee.
They shall speak of the glory of thy kingdom, and talk of thy power;
to make known to the sons of men his mighty acts, and the glorious
majesty of his kingdom. Thy kingdom *is* an everlasting kingdom, and
thy dominion *endureth* throughout all generations. (Ps. 145:1–13 KJV)

This joyful psalm speaks personally ("I will extol thee!") but not individualistically ("One generation shall praise thy works to another. . . .
All thy works shall praise thee . . . and thy saints shall bless thee!").
As we listen to the psalmist, before our mind's eye parade the mighty
works of God—actions and gifts that are publicly verifiable and that

also make a personal impact upon us, the recipients. God shows his
personal care through human persons, through David, through the
saints, and through the witness of one generation to another. While
the whole creation praises the Lord, each part in its own characteristic
manner, it is especially the role of human beings—of the saints—to
bless God!

The Personal God

In the last chapter, we considered how it is that God passes on to us,
through those who have known him before us, and who have seen him
more clearly for who he is, the greatest of gifts. This gift is not separate
from himself: for his greatest gift, made manifest in the Incarnation,
is everything that that divine action entailed. In his conception by
Mary through the Holy Spirit, in his humility and service, in his pas-
sion and death on the cross (a death that plunged deeply to the very
nadir of human experience), in the tomb, in his "preaching to the
souls in prison" (1 Pet. 3:19 EH), in the glorious resurrection, in the
victorious ascension, and in the sure promise that he will return, we
meet God-with-us in the person of Jesus. Nor is the centrality of the
person only a New Testament truth, though it came into full focus
and was enacted at the turn of the ages. Indeed, the interconnection
of our faith with the personal is intimated in the Old Testament time
and time again. There God not only reveals himself by means of the
unspeakable mysterious name of YHWH, the One who Is, but he is
also called "The God of your fathers, of Abraham, Isaac, and Jacob."
God's character comes into crystal-clear focus with the advent of
Jesus, when God takes on, or "assumes," humanity.

In this chapter we will think more deeply about the importance
of this personal center of our faith and see how Tradition is God's
personal gift, for he is the One from whom Holy Tradition originates.
This personal aspect of divine Tradition gives the chase to any fears
that we may harbor that what has been transmitted is rigid, stifling, or
repressive: for we have it on good report that the LORD "is not God of
the dead, but of the living" (Luke 20:38). Moreover, if God is himself
personal, then his way of working is also personal. As we have already

noticed, his major way of communicating to those who have blocked or impeded ears, his major way of shining forth to those whose eyes are veiled, is through *human persons*, made after his own image. We will, then, begin by thinking about the wonder of the living Tradition and how it reveals the personal God through persons to persons. In looking to the Scriptures and the early Christian writings for help with this, we will work through some of the passages that we have already considered and then fasten especially upon the Fourth Gospel. We will close by hearing again, via the incisive rendering of Patrick Reardon, the meditations of that classic Western theologian, the blessed Augustine: he insists that mediation is God's normative way with us, not because God does not want to reach us directly, but because his plan is to bind us together with each other, as we are bound also to him.

Up Close and Personal

It bears repeating that when we compare Christianity with its closest counterparts in world religions—that is, with Judaism and with Islam—Christianity differs in that it does not center first and foremost upon a book. The sacred page is very important, but it does not receive the same attention as Torah does in Judaism or as the Qur'an does in Islam. There is a saying among the rabbis that, though priestly service cannot be done in the Temple any more since the Temple has been destroyed, the one who studies Torah is accomplishing the same task. For Muslims, the Holy Qur'an is so sacred that it cannot even be translated: to be truly understood, it must be read as it was originally written.

But in the Christian understanding, God is different. Books can serve as testimonials to his greatness, can repeat the words that he has spoken, can record the visions by which he has appeared, and are even inspired, in-breathed by the Holy One. Yet God's people are called beyond study of God to God himself: it is *he* that is our home, and the Bible is one of the major ways to find that home. Moreover, God's Word is so pliable, so resilient, so able to go beyond, that it can be translated and still make its mark. The earliest Christians already had the Hebrew Scriptures in translation (the Greek Septuagint), and mainly used this Greek version in the formation of the New Testament. And there is another sign that God is not confined to the letters. Even the original New Testament speaks to us mainly in a second language used by the earliest Christians, only retaining a few of the Aramaic words that document its original cultural setting: it is written in Greek, not in the language that Jesus spoke during his ministry. God's choice of St. Paul, one who was a Roman citizen, who spoke Greek, but who studied Hebrew with the strictest sect known as the Pharisees, is a sign of this vitality that the Holy Spirit has bequeathed to the Church. Indeed, the essence of a *person*, if we are to go by the pattern set down by the tripersonal God, is to communicate beyond boundaries, reaching out to the other. Indeed, the central act of God in our midst, the Incarnation, shows us that God knows very well how to "translate" one thing—even *himself!*—into something else without a loss of integrity.

The Son comes among us as a person, in the sense that we normally understand the word, and as *the Person*, the new Adam and complete Human Being who gives meaning to the very idea of personhood. Hebrews, we recall, tells us: "In many and various ways God spoke of old to our fathers by the prophets; but in these last days he has spoken to us by his Son, whom he appointed the heir of all things, through whom also he created the world. He reflects the glory of God and bears the very stamp of his nature, upholding the universe by his word of power" (Heb. 1:1–3). In the variety of Old Testament writings, God spoke by persons to persons ("to our fathers [and mothers!] by the prophets"). But especially now we glimpse God's own personal character, for he speaks and acts in his Son, who bears the stamp of God's nature and whose own word is all-powerful. Words, spoken and written, are communicated from persons to persons. How could it be otherwise? For we are not bearing witness, in the first place, to a philosophy, a worldview, or an idea. Rather, we adore the incarnate Word, who is *the* Person, the true God-Man, Jesus our Lord. St. Paul, we remember, also spoke of the inner vitality of God's overtures to us:

> For what person knows those things that pertain to a human being except the spirit of the human that is in him? So also no one comprehends the thoughts of God except the Spirit of God. Now we have received not the spirit of the world, but the Spirit who is from God,

that we might understand the gifts bestowed on us by God. And we impart this in words not taught by human wisdom but taught by the Spirit, interpreting spiritual truths to those who possess the Spirit. (1 Cor. 2:11–13 EH)

When meeting a person, we are not simply dealing with a verbal message or a mental concept, but with someone who can be perceived in myriad ways and who makes an impact on all that is around. So, then, in the Scriptures, though they are composed of words for our ears, there is a good deal of emphasis upon the other senses as well, when we encounter God—images for our eyes as well as stimuli for our other faculties (such as smell and touch). Recall how Saul met Jesus in light and how in his writings he spoke to the Corinthians about "the light of the knowledge of the glory of God in the face of Christ" (2 Cor. 4:6). This same convert spoke about the very witness of the apostles as a kind of "odor," either an aroma of life for those who are being saved or a stench of death for those who reject Christ (2 Cor. 2:14–16). The Scriptures point us beyond their words and ideas to the living God, a God who took on flesh in a woman's womb, was plunged into the Jordan, and sang a hymn on the night of his betrayal. Indeed, this God who came into the realm of our senses often uses the presence of other human beings to point the way as well.

In chapter 2, we saw how one scholar, on hearing the opinion of Bishop Papias, considered that "oral tradition" was dying out at that time. However, this is only one way of interpreting what the second-century bishop had to say. This bishop himself wrote a volume that collected the words of the Lord. Though we have lost the whole work, we do have access to his preface through the report of the later historian Eusebius. It is there that Papias gives priority to the oral word and the tradition of interpretation that he received personally from the horses'—that is, the apostles' and elders'—mouths. He mentions that there are few of these first witnesses left, but his preference for the oral teaching of the apostles and of their disciples over the written memoirs (some of which became our four biblical Gospels) is astonishing to those of us who are Scripture oriented. Indeed, in gathering the traditions received from mouth to ear and putting them down on the written page, Papias carried on this verbal tradition in written form for the benefit of those who would not be able to hear these words from his own mouth. It is, however, still tradition, and it is a tradition that comes complete with interpretations:

> But I shall not hesitate also to put down for you along with my interpretations whatsoever things I have at any time learned carefully from the elders and carefully remembered, guaranteeing their truth. For I did not, like the multitude, take pleasure in those that speak much, but in those that teach the truth; not in those that relate strange commandments, but in those that deliver the commandments given by the Lord to faith, and springing from the truth itself. If, then, any one came, who had been a follower of the elders, I questioned him in regard to the words of the elders—what Andrew or what Peter said, or what was said by Philip, or by Thomas, or by James, or by John, or by Matthew, or by any other of the disciples of the Lord, and what things Aristion and the presbyter John, the disciples of the Lord, say. For I did not think that what was to be gotten from the books would profit me as much as what came from the living and abiding voice.[1]

This emphasis upon the oral word may seem counterintuitive to us, who might think with the commentator Clarke, whom we met in chapter 1, that something written down formally in a book would be more secure than a living voice. But Papias is confident of those whom Jesus' first apostles had taught and considered these traditions as though they were the very word and precept given by the Lord who is "the Truth itself." His reason is clear: he gives priority to a *living* voice!

As an example that will make this clear for us, let me tell you about how much I love to make pies. It is because I learned how to make pastry from my mother, an expert dessert-maker! There is something about the feel, the handling of the dough, the loving movement of the rolling pin that cannot be learned except by someone who knows what to do. You can't learn this technique well from a book—it is a kind of culinary tradition. The same is true of a subtle technique in playing, for example, the piano. One can look at diagrams of hands, with wrists down and up, and listen to the music, and perhaps approximate

---

1. Eusebius, *Ecclesiastical History* III, 39.3–4, in *Nicene and Post-Nicene Fathers*, Second Series, vol. 1, edited by Philip Schaff and Henry Wace and translated by Arthur Cushman McGiffert (Buffalo, NY: Christian Literature Publishing Co., 1890). Revised and edited for *New Advent* by Kevin Knight. http://www.newadvent.org/fathers/2501 .htm. Accessed January 2012.

a certain attack for a chord or a sustained arpeggio. It is much more satisfactory, however, to have the whole thing in three dimensions, with hearing, sight, and touch all combined before one's own person in the teacher who is showing and passing on this way of playing.

Papias' words, of course, were written prior to the time when the Church formally acknowledged together the writings that Christians would describe as "canonical"—that is, "according to the rule of faith."[2] Later, Christians would have a more established method of comparing spiritual things with things that merely seemed to be spiritual and would agree, more or less, regarding the extent of the holy books. However, Papias' confidence in the living voice of those who had been with the apostles serves as a check to our easy assumption that the Bible came first and that Tradition followed. Christians in his day had access to "the memoirs of the Apostles," and read them in liturgical services; they *also* listened attentively to those who had known the apostles, because the teaching came to them personally this way, through those who were "living letters," in the words of St. Paul (2 Cor. 3:3 EH). Persons encounter persons. Persons show forth Christ. Persons together make up the Church, the living body of Christ.

A word of clarification is required here. In using the word "person," we are not using the legal definition of "person," which is subject to

2. Normally we use the word "canon" as a way of referring to the collected works in the Bible, implying that these are in themselves "the rule" (Greek, *kanōn*) to be followed. Originally, however, the noun was not used to describe the inspired texts; only the adjective "canonical" was. That adjective can, of course, carry the meaning that the Scriptures are "rulish" or normative for us. It is far more likely, however, that when the lists of these "canonical" books were being hammered out by the early Church, the adjective was used as a way of declaring that in these books could be discerned the same "rule of faith or truth" (*regula fidei*; *kanōn tēs alētheias*) passed on by Jesus and the apostles. On this, see Fr. John Behr, *The Way to Nicea*, who points out that the purpose of the canon was not "so much to give fixed . . . statements" or "the literary hypothesis of Scripture" but to express "the correct hypothesis of Scripture itself." That is, neither doctrine nor the shape of the Biblical narrative is the center of the *regula fidei*, though these are important (and, I would argue, entailed in adherence to the canon). Rather, Scripture's own hypothesis, which puts forth Christ, must primarily be discerned; as such, true canonicity involves "a mode of interpretation delivered by the apostles in their proclamation of Christ" (35–37). Perhaps Fr. Behr's negative pronouncements are too absolute, but certainly the canon of truth implies a way of understanding the older covenant as proclaiming Jesus (though in a mysterious manner). We will consider Tradition and the rule of faith in a little more detail in the next chapter.

the vagaries of legal precedent and culture. Instead, we are defining the human person by looking at its prototype, Jesus the true Adam. Moreover, we are anticipating the hope that has been set before us, that all of us are meant to grow into the likeness of Christ, even though we are not fully persons yet. We who are so changeable will at last, as C. S. Lewis puts it, "have faces," and become *real* persons like Jesus himself.

The Three-Personal God and the God-Man

George Herbert, that exuberant and yet sober poet-priest of seventeenth-century England, understood well the very core of the gift that God has transmitted to us and its effect upon those who receive. In his characteristically irrepressible style, he exults in the twin gifts God has bequeathed to the Church but hints in the title that we are all-too-complacent about these gifts—indeed, "ungrateful":

> Thou hast but two rare cabinets full of treasure,
> The *Trinity*, and *Incarnation*:
> Thou hast unlockt them both,
> And made them jewels to betroth
> The work of thy creation
> Unto thy self in everlasting pleasure.[3]

How countercultural to speak of these central doctrines of the faith as treasure cabinets or *jewels,* indeed engagement tokens! Those outside the Church are more inclined to be either amused or annoyed at what are considered arcane dogmas; those inside pay lip service to them but frequently consider them either the product of ancient theologians writing in a different cultural context or mysteries that need to be placed on the shelf until we have eternal eyes to see them. But Herbert implies that these very actions of God, proclaimed by the Church in creed, hymn, and liturgy, are no mere indicators of orthodox theology but active in our lives. Indeed, it is exactly at those points in Scripture where we come face-to-face with the God-Man Jesus that we catch

3. George Herbert's "Ungratefullnesse" is a poem included in his collection *The Temple,* pages 1–189 of *The Poems of George Herbert from the Text of F. E. Hutchinson* (London: Oxford University Press, 1961), 73.

a glimpse of the Triune life and, indeed, may hear that Voice saying, "Come!" A similar yearning that ushers us into the presence of God is likewise inculcated when we read the luminous words of spiritual theologians, our older siblings in Christ, who have looked into the treasure chests opened to us by God and tried on the betrothal jewels for themselves.

Embedded, for example, like a jewel in both the Gospels of Matthew and Luke, there is a passage that has frequently puzzled scholars, for its language sounds to them far more in tune with what is called the "high Christology" of the Fourth Gospel. That is, Jesus shines forth as the Son in intimate communion with the Father, rather than simply as a fulfillment of the hopes and dreams of the Jewish people for a Messiah, an anointed one sent by God to give aid to Israel. In the previous chapter we looked at this passage as presenting the chains of reception whereby tradition comes to us. Let us look again, noticing now its translucent quality to show forth the divine Man and to intimate the mystery of the Holy Trinity, into whose company (astonishingly!) we are called. Here is truly a theological and spiritual jewel, set by Luke in a remarkable setting and fashioned as a tantalizing promise of intimacy with God. Notice especially the artistry of the passage, which moves in terms of a "chiastic" or envelope structure (ABCDC′B′A′), enshrining the mysterious and joyful message that Jesus here imparts to his followers:

A [H]e **said to them, "I saw** Satan fall like lightning from heaven.

B Behold, I have **given you** authority to tread upon serpents and scorpions, and over all the power of the enemy; and nothing shall hurt you.

C Nevertheless do not **rejoice** in this, that the **spirits** are subject to you;

D but rejoice that your names are written in heaven."

C′ In that same hour he **rejoiced** in the Holy **Spirit**

B′ and said, "I thank thee, Father, Lord of heaven and earth, that thou hast hidden these things from the wise and understanding and revealed them to babes; yea, Father, for such was thy gracious will.

All things **have been given** over to me by my Father; and no one knows who the Son is except the Father, or who the Father is except the Son and anyone to whom the Son chooses to reveal him."

A′ Then turning **to the disciples he said** privately, "Blessed are the eyes which see **what you see!**"

(Luke 10:18–23)[4]

Jesus begins by speaking about what *he* has seen and ends by impressing upon his disciples the solemn significance of what *they* have seen. Within these bookends, the B sections speak about authority, which he has given to the disciples over the enemy and all authority that the Father has given to him, the Son. The second B section is extended, for it is explaining the inner mystery of the Holy Trinity, and how it is that the authority and knowledge of the Son have been given to those who, on the surface, are "babes" and simple ones. The implication is that it is because of the special relationship between Father and Son (and Holy Spirit) that the disciples can be included within God's will. Within these frames are the C sections, in which Jesus tells the disciples not to rejoice that they have authority over (evil) *spirits*, and in which Jesus himself rejoices greatly in the *Holy Spirit* because of what God is doing and showing. In the midst of this is buried the command (D): "Rejoice that your names are written in heaven." Just as there is intimate communion between the Father and the Son, so the disciples, indeed their very names, have a special place in heaven: the communion of the Father, Son, and Holy Spirit have made a place for them, a place where they can know the mystery of God and his will. Jesus, in harmony with the Holy Spirit, tells them that no one knows the Father, that most mysterious Person and Source of all, except himself and those to whom he, the Son, reveals the will and mystery of the Father. Then he implies, speaking even more privately to the disciples, that this is happening at that very moment, for their eyes are blessed.

On the basis of this passage alone, the reader cannot assume that this blessing will extend beyond the privileged disciples—unless,

---

4. The version followed here is, for the most part, the RSV. I have altered this version slightly to show Greek root parallels in the wording and formatted to enhance the parallelism.

perhaps, one hears Jesus' statement about revelation to "babes" in a general sense and detects a programmatic tone in his words concerning the knowledge of the Father vouchsafed to "*any one* to whom the Son chooses to reveal him" (Luke 10:22). Yet it is no imposition upon the text to generalize Jesus' statement, applying it to the faithful community as a whole. After all, the disciples and the seventy have just returned from a mission, directed by Jesus, in which they have been told to proclaim the nearness of God's rule. Moreover, Luke's entire scheme, both in the Gospel and in the Acts, is to show that this reign and this overturning of the evil one are for the benefit of all of Israel. Indeed, the One who rules and overturns is at the same time a light to the gentiles—beginning in Jerusalem and Judea, then Samaria, then to the ends of the world (Acts 1:6; cf. Acts 2:39). The "names written in heaven," then, go beyond Jesus' inner circle, as we see also in Jesus' solemn words in that other spiritual Gospel, John.

Here too words about the personal calling and intimate communion of God with those whom he has called are framed within a discussion of those heavenly things not clearly seen—the fellowship between Father, Son, and Holy Spirit. Jesus has come into his world, to his own, and on that last night before his costliest gift, he addresses his Father in the earshot of those who will soon be confused and grief stricken:

> Father, the hour has come; glorify your Son so that the Son may glorify you, since you have given him power over all humanity, to give eternal life to all whom you have given to him. And this is eternal life, that they know you the only true God, and Jesus Christ whom you have sent. Seeing that I have accomplished the work that you gave me to do, I have glorified you on earth; and now, Father, glorify me in your own presence with the glory which I had with you before the world was made. I have manifested thy name to the ones whom you gave me out of the world; yours they were, and you gave them to me, and they have kept your word. Now they know that everything that you have given me is from you; *for I have given them the words that you gave me, and they have received them and know in truth that I have come from your side*; and they have believed that you sent me. I am praying for them . . . for they are yours; all mine is yours, and yours are mine, and I am glorified in them. . . . I am not praying only for these ones, but also for those who believe in me through their word, that they may all be one; even as you, Father, are in me, and I in you, that they also

may be in us, so that the world may believe that thou hast sent me. The glory that you have given me I have given to them, that they may be one even as we are one, I in them and you in me, that they may become perfectly one, so that the world may know that you have sent me and have loved them even as you have loved me. Father, I desire that those also, whom you have given me, may be with me where I am, to behold my glory which you have given to me in your love for me before the foundation of the world. (John 17:1–24 EH)

Here we see quite clearly the element of Holy Tradition passed on: Jesus repeats a persistent theme throughout John, that he is doing, specifically, what the Father has told him to do (5:19; 10:37) when he gives to the disciples the *words*—or perhaps *the things*—of God. The disciples have received these traditions, and in so doing they have come to understand that Jesus has himself been transmitted to them from the Father's side: he has given (*didōmi*), they have received (*lambanō*), and they know that he has come to them from the side of (*para*) the Father. (Let us recall *paradidōmi* and *paralambanō*, those active and passive technical words associated with transmission and reception of tradition: here all the composites of these words are used to describe what Jesus' followers have received from the Father through his Son.) The "words" or "things" come as part and parcel of God's greatest gift given over to them—the Son.

We encounter, then, not merely a chain of reception but a divine action that changes the very character of those who open their arms and hearts to the Gift. As Jesus said to his disciples at the very beginning of this his final teaching, "No longer do I call you servants, for the servant does not know what his master is doing; but I have called you friends, for all that I have heard from my Father I have made known to you" (15:15). So changed will their character be that ultimately they will come to share in the very glory of the Son, who is with the Father. As Jesus will be glorified in them, so they will be glorified in him—and not them only but also those who believe because of the original apostles. The giving and receiving of this gift will render all concerned *one*, in a divine sense that goes beyond any mere human harmony. Because what—or rather, Whom—is being received is the Person of persons, the God-Man, he transfigures those who embrace this holiest Tradition, this One who has been given to and for the world.

Grace Is Not a Substance

We see very clearly in these passages from Luke and John the deep intercommunion between Father and Son—but what of the Holy Spirit? We have seen this Person of the Trinity lurking in the margins of Jesus' words with regard to the disciples' joy: he rejoiced *in the Holy Spirit* (Luke 10:21). Those who know the whole script of Jesus' words to his disciples on his last fateful night will remember also that the Holy Spirit is explicitly introduced by Jesus there (John 14:17, 26; 15:26; 16:13). However, it is not until later that the disciples come to understand this Person, by whom the transformation is accomplished within them, and who turns teachings that they have received from Jesus into life-giving Holy Tradition for the entire body of Christ. In John's Gospel, at the very minute when Jesus dies, we hear him say "It is finished" and are told that he "traditioned" (the word is *paradidōmi*) the Spirit (19:30). Some translators read this as simply a quaint way of referring to the separation of soul and body (and this surely is implied), but it would seem that far more is at stake. To give the Spirit is, indeed, the fulfillment of God's work in the world, for with that gift humans become what God intends for them to be. When we move one chapter further, to the dénouement of the Fourth Gospel, we are able to see the full significance of the giving over of the Spirit. Here, Jesus appears to the disciples after the resurrection and does a very strange thing: in a scene that recalls God's activity in Genesis 2, he "breathes" upon them, and says to them, "Receive [the verb is *lambanō*] the Holy Spirit" (John 20:22). Now what the first human had being received was not "spirit" (Hebrew *ruach*; Greek *pneuma*) but simply "soul" or "life-force" (Hebrew *nephesh*; Greek *psychē*). And here the evangelist speaks not merely "spirit" but the "Holy Spirit." The apostles are not merely empowered but are here infused with the very Person of whom Jesus had said, he "will be in you" (14:17) and "will take what is mine and declare it to you" (16:14). Jesus gives the Holy Spirit—the gift of God himself, among his people and vivifying them.

In Acts, we receive the account of how this same One, promised by Jesus, visited and visibly transformed the entire host of believers on Pentecost, so that they could take the things and words of Jesus and pass them on to those who were in Jerusalem and "far off" (Acts

2:39). In Acts, as well as in John, the themes of holiness, Tradition, the Holy Spirit, fellowship, glory, and unity with the Triune God come together. Everywhere we look, the things of God come to human beings by means of the God-Man and through the ministration of the Holy Spirit, transforming them into a living community energized by God himself. They do not receive a discrete gift, or a grace, separate from God—they receive the Son, and then the Holy Spirit, and so are gathered into the fellowship shared by Father, Son, and Spirit. In the reception, and in the gathering, they are transfigured.

Some theologians speak of "grace" as a kind of substance or abstract principle with which God blesses his people or by which we are forgiven. Instead, the Gospels show us how God actually entrusts us with himself—with the Son, whose very rejection was transformed into our acceptance, and with the Holy Spirit, who by his very reticence or reserve shows forth the glory of Jesus among God's people (cf. John 16:13).

Mediation and the Immediate God

God put his plan into action and made his transforming impact upon the world, upon us, in person. We should surely expect that he should continue in his customary fashion, using persons, as indeed Jesus intimated in his prayer—"I pray also for those who believe because of their word" (John 17:30 EH). Everywhere we look in the New Testament, we see how the God who has come to us in an immediate way—in his own Person, in Jesus, and in the Holy Spirit—continues to work through human persons. They do what Jesus did and what they are taught to do by the Spirit. We see this in works as distinct as 1 Corinthians, Acts, James, Jude, and 2 Peter. Some of the interconnections traced between faithful persons and others are, indeed, challenging to our individualistic ears. For example, what does a contemporary Christian make of St. Paul's strange question, "How do you know, wife, whether you will save your husband? Or how do you know, husband, whether you will save your wife?" (1 Cor. 7:16 EH). Such passages were extremely off-putting to me when I was a much younger Christian. I was used to hearing, while wearing my quaint Salvation

Army uniform (complete with nineteenth-century bonnet) on the evening streets of Toronto, that good-natured but mocking chorus, "Salvation Army, save my soul. Send me to heaven in a sugar bowl!" to which I customarily retorted, "We don't save anybody. That is the work of the Lord Jesus!"

Well, who was right? St. Paul's challenge to the believing spouse, or twenty-first-century reserved-evangelical sensibilities? I suppose it depends, partially, on how the word "save" is being used. If we use the word "salvation" in the strictest sense of referring to the coming of the Son in the flesh, to his act of atonement, and to the redemption and release found in the cross, descent to hell, and resurrection, then this is, of course, the unique act of our Lord. However, *sōtēria*, or salvation, means "wholeness," and it is clear that all of us who are in Christ are called to act for the spiritual well-being of others. Moreover, the acts of salvation, the mighty acts of the Lord, involved others from beginning to end—the Mother of the Lord, who said "yes" to God's message through Gabriel, the women at the tomb who (as one ancient song puts it) "cast away the ancestral curse" to tell the apostles the good news, the apostles who spoke of it in Jerusalem and abroad, Ananias who explained the way to that Pharisee Saul who had abruptly seen the Lord, that same St. Paul who wrote letters that have explained the way for innumerable Christians, and the followers of the disciples who listened and researched (cf. Luke 1:1) so as to transmit the truth to us. The mediation is ongoing!

Nor is it merely a matter of the passing on of words. To return to St. Paul's description of the family, we may be even more puzzled to see how the apostle describes the inevitable result of a Christian presence there, even if it is only one of the spouses. He frowns on separation in the case of an already established (but mixed) marriage, saying, "For the unbelieving husband is made holy because of his wife, and the unbelieving wife is made holy because of her husband. Otherwise your children would be unclean, but as it is, they are holy" (1 Cor. 7:14 ESV). This is truly odd! Perhaps we might have limited his challenge "How do you know if you might not save your husband/wife" to a scenario in which the godly spouse teaches, or leads, the other to a saving knowledge of the Lord. But here, the effect seems, well, more *organic*. The very fact that a Christian is joined to another simply makes its impact. In some way, the other is "holy" or "set apart"—already he or she is in contact with the holy presence of God through the presence of the one with whom that spouse is intimate. And in case some are predisposed to argue with him, he says something he expects the Corinthians to acknowledge—"for, of course, your children are not illegitimate and unclean, are they?" In one sense, Paul is arguing that these are true marriages and that the children have not been conceived out of wedlock—perhaps there were some who, like the Roman Catholic teaching today, were arguing that when a person becomes a Christian, the previous tie that they have made with a nonbeliever is qualified and can, in some cases, be annulled. But the language seems more extravagant than this, speaking about "holiness" as something that has a quasi-magnetic or infectious quality. This is confirmed by his later question regarding whether the spouse might not be actually saved. So it is not that the "holiness" imparted leads to automatic acceptance by God—this is not a magic or mechanical process. But the presence of a Christian, energized by the Holy Spirit, in the life of an unbeliever is nothing to sneeze at: it may well make a permanent mark, and most certainly has an impact upon the children of such a marriage. Here, it would seem, Christians are being understood as having the same strange effect that Jesus had: when he came into contact with the "unclean" of his day (lepers and so on) he was not contaminated but made them clean.[5]

We meet the same paradox in other passages that deal with the solid and real effect of believers upon others, while still maintaining the importance of personal choice and acceptance on the part of those affected. So, for example, James speaks about the reality of mediation and dependence, even while forbidding a magical view of grace:

> But above all . . . do not swear, either by heaven or by earth or with any other oath, but let your yes be yes and your no be no, so that you might not fall under [God's] judgment. . . . Is any among you sick? Let that one call for the elders of the church, and let them pray over him

5. Other teaching makes it clear, however, that Christians are not to deliberately marry non-Christians with the hope of giving them this "good infection." Elsewhere St. Paul is very clear about the dangers of marrying outside the faith, even while he gives this explicit instruction to new converts whose spouses have not joined them (yet) in the Way.

(or her), anointing the sick person with oil in the name of the Lord; and the prayer of faith will save the sick one, and the Lord will raise him (or her) up; and if (s)he has committed sins, (s)he will be forgiven. Therefore confess your sins to one another, and pray for one another, that you may be healed. The prayer of a righteous one has great power in its effects. Elijah was a human of like nature with us and he prayed earnestly that it would not rain, and for three years and six months it did not rain on the earth. Then he prayed again and the heaven gave rain, and the earth yielded its fruit. My brothers (and sisters), if any among you wanders from the truth and someone brings that one back, may that one be assured that whoever brings back a sinner from the way of his or her wandering will save that one's soul from death and will cover a multitude of sins. (James 5:12–19 EH)

So, then, there is no point in "swearing" by religious things, thinking that such an oath has magical powers. We should have a simple and straightforward way of thinking about life and also of acting. Nevertheless, our communion with one another possesses a mysterious quality—confession and prayer can lead to miraculous healing, as can anointing with oil. Prayer can make an impact upon the earth and upon others. And though each person is responsible for his or her own answer to God, and for his or her conduct—a sinner wanders in his or her own way—still it is possible for a brother or sister to intervene and so participate in that person's salvation. God works through oil, prayer, words, and love—through the material and the audible, and through unseen realities as well. Above all, he works upon persons by persons, and normatively through those who have been set aside (that is, the elders) in the Church.

A similar picture is given in Acts:

And wonders—not of the ordinary kind!—God performed by the hands of Paul, so that handkerchiefs or aprons were carried away from his body to those that were ill and diseases were released out of them and the evil spirits came out of them. Then some of the itinerant Jewish exorcists set their hand at pronouncing the name of the Lord Jesus over those who had evil spirits, saying, "I adjure you by that Jesus whom Paul proclaims." (There were seven sons of a Jewish high priest named Sceva doing this.) But the evil spirit answered them, "Jesus I know, and Paul I understand; but who are you?" And the man in whom was the evil spirit assaulted them, mastered all of them, and overpowered them, so that they ran out of that house naked and wounded. And this became known to all the inhabitants of Ephesus, Jews and Greeks; and fear fell upon them all; and the name of the Lord Jesus was magnified. Many also of those who were now faithful came, confessing and acknowledging their practices. And a significant number of those who practiced magic arts brought their books together and burned them before everyone; and when they counted the value of these, they found it came to fifty thousand pieces of silver. In this way, the word of the Lord grew and became strong. (Acts 19:11–20 EH)

In this strange story we see the juxtaposition of miracle, or mighty deed of God, over against miracle, as well as the presence of human influence for the faith alongside personal responsibility to receive it. An "ordinary kind" of wonder, in the view of even the scriptural writings, would have involved a direct contact of the miracle worker with the one to be healed. We hear of this in both the story of Naaman, who anticipates that Elisha should come out and wave his hand ritually so that he would be healed (2 Kings 5:11), and indirectly in Jesus' response to the remarkable faith of the centurion, who accepted that Jesus' word alone would suffice, whereas others expected something more dramatic (Matt. 8:7–10). In the case of Paul, God's transforming power was so palpable that even personal items of clothing had been affected and could be used to transmit God's healing. This was evidently seen as some kind of trick by the seven sons of Sceva, who knew nothing of the true identity of the Lord Jesus and understood nothing of the type of sanctity shown by Paul. For them, it was a matter of technique, a mechanical matter—and they are soon disabused of this! The crowd, it seems, understands clearly this lesson concerning the difference between this mechanical view of salvation or healing and what the gospel of Jesus entails, for they are convicted of their superstitious ways and confess them openly before the believing community, becoming members themselves. Here we see that God's ways involve the physical, especially those objects associated with one of his children, but not mere ritual words. The exorcists err in thinking that they can control God but are told by the demons that the names of Jesus and Paul are more than mere magical formulae or transporters of ideas that can be learned through a chain by rote—they are persons who offer true communion and thorough healing. And so the true healing, for those with ears to hear and eyes to see, whether Jew or gentile, takes place in community: they confessed before all. A similar dynamic is seen in the short epistle of Jude:

> But you must remember, beloved, the predictions of the apostles of our Lord Jesus Christ; they said to you, "In the last time there will be scoffers, following their own ungodly passions." It is these who set up divisions, worldly people, devoid of the Spirit. But you, beloved, build yourselves up on your most holy faith; pray in the Holy Spirit; keep yourselves in the love of God; wait for the mercy of our Lord Jesus Christ unto eternal life. And convince some, who doubt; save some, by snatching them out of the fire; on some have mercy with fear, hating even the garment spotted by the flesh. Now to him who is able to keep you from falling and to present you without blemish before the presence of his glory with rejoicing, to the only God, our Savior through Jesus Christ our Lord, be glory, majesty, dominion, and authority, before all time and now and forever. Amen. (Jude 17–25)

Here, cheek by jowl, we find instructions that are personal and corporate. "Build yourselves up" by means of prayer, care, and attentiveness is followed by injunctions to "convince" doubters and even "save some." Indeed, those who wait for the mercy of Jesus will be evident, over against the scoffers of the age, through their action of showing mercy to the weak while maintaining an apt reverence for, or fear of the dangers inherent in, engaging in such spiritual battle. There is both a responsibility for each Christian to mind his or her own affairs and for each to care about others who are in dire circumstances. Over all of this is the assurance that the real strength for the Church is not in human edification or rescue but in "the only God" who is both Savior and Preserver, the One who is able to keep his Church from falling. Such salvation—whether initial or ongoing—is a real hope but does not take place automatically, without God's regard for human participation. His is the energy, and so we are enjoined to both acknowledge this and to act accordingly, whether we have our own safety in view or that of others.

One final example will suffice, a passage to which we have had recourse already—the first chapter of 2 Peter. In chapter 3 of this study we noticed that the apostle puts forward the apostolic witness to the transfigured Jesus and the apostolic interpretation of the Old

Testament as the lamp of the Church, all the while looking forward to
the day when the promised Lord Jesus will return to us in full glory:

> We have established as more secure the prophetic word [of the Old
> Testament]. To this you will do well to pay attention as to a light shin-
> ing in a dark place, until the day dawns and the morning star rises in
> your hearts. (2 Pet. 1:19 EH)

Because the Church is a body, and because the Holy Spirit speaks to all
of God's people, neither prophecy nor the reading of Scripture is an
individualistic affair. Rather, both are actions performed in the body
of the Church and with special reference to the apostles, who learned
from the Lord Jesus: "No prophecy of Scripture opens itself automatically to interpretation" (2 Pet. 1:20 EH). As part of this corporate life,
however, there is also a word to each and to all about growth in holiness.
After his initial reference to abundant grace, peace, and knowledge,
the apostle goes on to explain how these things belong to the Church:

> Just so, all things that have to do with life and godliness are yours
> through the divine power, through the knowledge of that One who
> called us to his own splendor and excellence, by which he has given us
> his priceless and very great promises. These were given so that through
> them you might become sharers in the divine nature, while fleeing from
> the corruption that is in the world because of passion. *And because of
> these very things*, make every effort to add to your faith excellence, to
> knowledge self-control, to self-control endurance, to endurance godli-
> ness, to godliness familial affection, and to affection divine love. For
> as these things belong to you multiply, they establish you in the full
> knowledge of our Lord Jesus Christ, so that you are neither ineffective
> nor unfruitful. Indeed, whoever lacks these things is blind and short-
> sighted and has forgotten the cleansing from his or her former sins.
> Therefore . . . make every effort to confirm your call and election, for
> if you do this you will never fall. Thus, an entrance into the everlasting
> kingdom of our Lord and Savior Jesus Christ will be richly provided for
> you. Therefore I intend always to remind you of these things, though
> you know them and are established in the truth that has come to you. I
> consider it right, as long as I am in this earthly tabernacle of my body,
> to energize you through this remembrance, since I know that the putting
> off of my tent will come soon, as our Lord Jesus Christ revealed to me.
> But I am making every effort to ensure that after my exodus you will
> keep the memory of these things. (2 Pet. 1:3–15 EH)

Throughout this extended introduction there is an interplay between God's action and human action, between the apostle's action and what he hopes will be the action of those who hear his words. *Because* all has been given by God, they are to make a concerted effort. They have been called and elected, yet are called to make this certain by growing in virtues. They know these things already, yet the apostle considers it appropriate to remind them: indeed, the very remembrance is a catalyst to their growth, just as memory was a key component of the witness of the apostles, who recalled what Jesus had said and done.[6] His own life and actions he sees as a mirror of that of the Lord Jesus and believes that this is also the calling of those whom he encourages. The apostle describes his embodied condition, saying that he finds himself now in a body that is a mere "tent," which he must put off (2 Pet. 1:13). He also implies that he is called to the radiance of Christ and will, like Jesus, undergo an "exodus" (the literal meaning of "departure," 2 Pet. 1:15) just as his Lord looked forward to a departure (again, literally "exodos," Luke 9:31) during the Transfiguration event (which he will recall for them in vv. 16–18). As for the recipients of his letter, they have already been visited by the "arriving truth" (2 Pet. 1:12 EH), the truth "that has arrived for them." This very word for "arriving" reminds us of the technical term used for the visitation of the Lord, *parousia*, a term applied to both his first and his promised coming. Similarly, they are guaranteed an "entrance into" (*eisodos*, literally "road into") the eternal glorious kingdom (2 Pet. 1:11), just as the apostles entered the glory cloud on Mount Tabor (Luke 9:34). Yet they are dependent upon the apostles for the earthly witness, for these leaders were with Jesus on the holy mountain and can testify to it (2 Pet. 1:19).

Everywhere, then, there is an interplay between God's action and human action, a kind of tension between the sovereign actions of the Lord, who comes and calls and shines, and the responsiveness of the Church. Within the Christian body too there is an interplay between the apostles and those who hear their words; there is both a corporate

---

6. On the importance of memory, the unfortunate marginalization of that activity in twentieth-century reconstructions of the formation and reception of gospel traditions (cf. form critical studies) and the slow recognition of memory as a key factor in New Testament studies, see Alan Kirk, "Social and Cultural Memory," 1–24.

nature to be discerned in the Church, and a personal responsibility for each member to be responsive to the apostolic tradition. The faithful already possess the riches; they will gain more if they are reminded about these truths. Though God has acted, this is not a call to be passive but to be active, so that the faithful are eagerly seeking, or "making every effort," as the apostle both models this for them and calls them to it. Meditation, intercession, and apostolic activity are a strong part of God's modus operandi. Yet human activity neither diminishes the impact of the radiant Lord upon each member of the Church nor serves as a substitute for each member's own action within the Christian body. Paul states this double mystery to the Philippians: "work out your [plural] own salvation with fear and trembling; for God is at work in you [plural], both to will and to work for his good pleasure" (Phil. 2:12b–13). Somehow, then, mediation and the immediate presence of God do not cancel each out, nor are they at war. Each of us has a role to play, but all is of God himself. Our integrity as the Church depends on each bearing his or her own burden, but all of us bearing the burdens of others. How would we expect otherwise, given the glimpse that we have been vouchsafed concerning the Holy Trinity—each Person divine, yet all three one God? This corporate yet personal dynamic has been delightfully traced for us by Fr. Patrick Reardon, who revisits a famous passage written by the blessed Augustine of Hippo—namely Augustine's preface of *On Christian Doctrine*. Fr. Patrick passes on the wisdom of that ancient theologian, who notes "the Lord's reluctance . . . to deal with people one-to-one, bypassing the normal forms of human mediation." Following the bishop of Hippo, he cites the deacon Philip's interventions with the Ethiopian pilgrim, St. Peter's intervention with Cornelius, and, most spectacularly, St. Paul's concourse with Ananias. When Saul inquires, having been accosted by the Lord in a vision, what he is to do, he receives an unexpected response:

> Jesus asserts, in effect, "I refuse to say another word to you, Saul of Tarsus. Get yourself into Damascus and consult those people you were on your way to persecute. You humble your soul to the authority of My Church, because your ill treatment of those Christians was inflicted on Me. I will not deal with you directly. Those people in Damascus speak for Me." . . . [T]o instruct men directly . . . would betray . . .

man's corporate nature, which is also the condition of the church. . . .
[W]rote Augustine, "love itself, which ties men together in the bond of
unity, would have no means of pouring soul into soul, and, as it were,
mingling them to one another, if men never learned anything from
their fellow men." (*De Doctrina Christiana*, Preface, 6)[7]

We close this consideration of God's personal gift with those remarkable words of the elder John, who reminds us of the concourse that
believers have both with each other and with the Triune Lord through
the Holy Spirit. Do these words speak about the ineluctable presence
of the Lord, or of the importance of human response to the Word
of Life? Do these words speak about the apostolic proclamation, or
about the common gift shared by all in the body? Do they present an
immediate shining of the light into our world, or do they imply the
importance of apostolic mediation? Or are these false alternatives?

> That which was from the beginning, which we have heard, which we
> have seen with our eyes, which we have looked upon and touched with
> our hands, concerning the word of life—the life was made manifest,
> and we saw it, and testify to it, and proclaim to you the eternal life
> which was with the Father and was made manifest to us—that which
> we have seen and heard we proclaim also to you, so that you may
> have communion with us; and our communion is with the Father and
> with his Son Jesus Christ. And we are writing this that our joy may
> be complete. (1 John 1:1–4 RSV alt.)

7. Fr. Patrick Reardon, "Pastoral Ponderings."

–6–

HOLY TRADITION
VERSUS HUMAN TRADITIONS

Discerning the Difference Today

Throughout this study we have tried to understand what the Bible says concerning tradition—a somewhat difficult quest given the historical complexities and translational challenges encountered by twenty-first-century Christians. We have faced our cultural ambivalence, the bias in some English translations, and the legacy of the Roman/Reformed debate that continues to color this conversation. We have noted that it is too simplistic merely to associate tradition with the elements of Church life and teaching that were spoken and heard rather than written. Further, we have recalled how both spoken and written traditions informed the Scriptures, both Old Testament (as we think of the formation of the Hebrew Bible via the sages and rabbis) and New (as we remember the apostolic era). During the time that the books of the New Testament were being composed, the Church interpreted the revelation of Jesus Christ in the light of the Old Testament and paid special attention to other, unwritten, apostolic traditions. Moreover, as the Church has developed, traditions have sprung from the reading and interpretation of Scriptures, some ephemeral and time-particular, but others deeply rooted and persistent today.

Scripture and tradition, then, are at every step interwoven—in their prehistory, in the process of writing and compiling, and in the ongoing acts of reading and interpreting. This dynamic is underscored both in Paul's letters and in 2 Peter, where the spoken word as well as the written word is described as authoritative. It is not whether they are spoken or written that renders words authoritative on the one hand or "deadly" on the other. Rather, the difficulty seems to come when those who receive them forget that truthful words are not ends in themselves nor objects of worship. In contrast, honest words find their reliability when they are uttered in relationship to the One who is the Word; they are meant to point to or illuminate him.

At every turn, the personal dimension is involved. Our tripersonal and Holy God uses persons, both humble and of higher repute, to ensure that the divine gifts are passed on and received. Especially the apostolic witness shines forth, though the apostles themselves speak of the gifts that they receive from others in the Church. Here is no rigid ladder of command but a dynamic that both establishes the authority of those first witnesses and also yields surprises, as the Holy Spirit uses whom he desires. God gives the gift of himself, in the Son and the Holy Spirit: he moves immediately into our midst but also is interpreted to us as the Spirit uses our brothers and sisters for the good of each and for all. The Father has "given over" the Son into the hands of humanity; the Son has "traditioned" the Holy Spirit to us.

Since tradition has taken such an honorable place in the life of the Church, can we therefore say that *every* practice that we have inherited is part and parcel of what can be called "Holy Tradition"—Tradition that is "holy" and thus separate from all other human traditions in its scope and its permanency? Surely not, or the letter to the Colossians would not warn, "Beware in case someone takes you captive through philosophy and empty deceit, according to the tradition of humans, after the elements of the world, and not according to Christ" (Col. 2:8 EH). Of course, some of those philosophies may be evil in themselves, but many of the human traditions tackled in the New Testament served a good purpose at the right time and are criticized not for their essence but for overreaching themselves—even the written Torah, we have seen, falls into this category. So then, both St. Paul (or his disciple) in Colossians and the Lord himself in Mark 7 imply that there is a distinction between that which must at all costs be conserved and those things that serve penultimate purposes and so are by nature mutable. In the case of Colossians, there is some debate among commentators about which distorted "traditional" things the apostle is targeting: some have suggested that his use of the participle *sylagōgōn* ("taking [you] captive") is a pun upon the noun synagogue, and that, whatever other strange ideas and practices might have been promoted by those bothering the faithful in Colossae, these were bound up with an exaggerated view of the Torah. In the case of Jesus' debate with the Pharisees (Mark 7), the point is clear—the rabbinic hedge placed around Torah, originally conceived to prevent sin, has obscured it so that Torah has been robbed of its original purpose—to point to the living God. In his second letter to the Corinthians, St. Paul expands upon this problem, showing that the Torah itself came to have only a ministry of *death* rather than life among those whose eyes were blinded to the true Image, Jesus (2 Cor. 3–4).

Tradition, Freedom, and Commitment

If even holy Torah, transmitted by the angelic hand (Acts 7:53; Gal. 3:19) to Moses, could be rendered inoperative, could become a stone of stumbling (cf. Rom. 9:30–32), then other traditions are even more liable to misuse. In our spiritual life, we are witnesses and receivers both in the large picture, going back to the apostles, and at a smaller range, as members of particular communities with particular received traditions. Yet our identity as receivers is complicated by the Christian conviction that we are no longer merely servants to obey commands or juvenile students who must dutifully parrot what we have been taught (cf. Gal. 3:24). Rather, we are friends and heirs brought into the very counsel of God through the Holy Spirit in the Church. In 1520, Martin Luther memorialized this interplay between freedom and service in his two propositions of *The Freedom of a Christian*:

> A Christian is a perfectly free lord of all, subject to none.
> A Christian is a perfectly dutiful servant of all, subject to all.

In attitude and practice, those following Luther have frequently emphasized the first proposition to the detriment of the second. Let us return to those Pauline verses over which Luther pored in the composition of his couplet:

> But thanks be to God, that you who were once slaves of sin have become obedient from the heart to the pattern of teaching to which you were handed over, and having been freed from sin, you became "slaves" to righteousness. (I speak in human terms because of the weakness of our human condition.) (Rom. 6:17–19b EH)

Here we find a conjunction of freedom and service and also an intriguing use of the technical term *paradidōmi,* interconnected with the phrase "mold" (Greek, *typos*) or "pattern of teaching." Paul has in mind traditional teaching in the Church and understands this not only as a body of doctrine but as an actual type, mold, pattern, or strategy of understanding and practice to which the Roman Christians have become obedient from the heart and not simply as a formality. This mode or pattern of teaching has become part of the internal DNA of the Church. Admitting that he is using an unusual metaphor ("I speak in human terms"), he likens not only their former situation under sin but also their present circumstance to a "slavery," since they have "been given over" to a way of living and thinking, that is, to a tradition. We might expect that the apostle would say that the pattern of teaching had been committed *to them,* but instead he reverses the statement in order to underscore the submission or indebtedness of the new Christians.

We may be tempted to translate verse 17, "you have become obedient to the pattern of teaching *to which you have been committed*"; however, today's subjective use of the term "commitment" would then trick us into thinking that this is merely an individual choice made initially by the new Christians as they commit themselves to the apostolic teaching. This is not exactly what Paul means, though indeed he is concerned for voluntary service from the heart. His metaphor is more jolting. His word choice implies that they have been "handed over" like a slave, or "traditioned" like apprentices to the pattern of teaching, so that they are now under submission to righteousness. Two scenarios emerge. One is the picture of the Romans as themselves a part of God's own living tradition (they are themselves "traditioned"), embodying that prayer for unity that Jesus prayed concerning those whom the Father gave to him (John 17:6). The other is that they, like Jesus, have been "handed over" (John 19:16) as slaves, as those bound to obedience, so that they become actual participants in Christ's submissive life and death.

Whichever picture St. Paul has in mind here (and it may be both) he goes on to call on his readers to "turn over" (6:19 uses another *para* word in the Greek) the members of their body for the purposes of being made holy. The point is clear: choice and committed service are intertwined, and in the same way all the people of God are linked in this ongoing process of transmitting the tradition and of incorporation together into the life of Christ. In speaking about their *belonging* to the pattern of teaching, as apprentices or even slaves, Paul refers to something far more august and more stable than mere human traditions. We are on the verge of discovering an apostolic reference to what will come to be known in the Church as Holy Tradition with a capital *T*—a pattern to be followed, a way of reading Scripture, a lifestyle, a belief, and a mind-set that are part and parcel of holiness and the "making of many righteous" (Rom. 5:19 EH).

In the very letter that argues for freedom from the Torah for gentile Christians (Galatians), the apostle surprisingly pronounces a benediction upon those who "follow this rule (*kanōn*)," upon the followers whom he also names "the [true] Israel of God" (Gal. 6:16 EH). Freedom and a "rule" are not at enmity but come together in the Christian Way. Elsewhere, the apostle is careful to make a distinction between which teaching comes "from the Lord" and which has come from his own reasoning process. Dealing with the nitty-gritty of Church affairs, he labels carefully which commands are "of the Lord" (1 Cor. 7:10) and which come from himself, by the Spirit (1 Cor. 7:12; 25, 40b). The way that he couches his judgments in the latter cases make it clear that he does not consider these immutable commands, though he does appeal to solid theological principles, the inspiration of the Spirit, and devotion to the Lord as he explains them.

We should expect, then, to find evidence in the life of the Church that some traditions undergo change or modification. Where we do find changes, moreover, we cannot explain these only in terms of the putting aside of a briefly held practice or merely a change of culture among God's people. Instead, we shall see that some of these modifications are theological in nature, and that the original tradition indeed had deep roots in the history of the Church. Let us take as examples four of these "hard cases," trying to discern why Christians sometimes felt free to "sit loose" to what they had originally received. Our cases are quite disparate in focus or topic—the apostles' use of an Old Testament prophecy, some New Testament authors' alteration of religious observance, the later Church's application of an apostolic and New Testament decree, and the classical Church's worship of the Holy Spirit as it came to understand the Holy Trinity. Once we have examined these historical test cases, we will consider briefly several of today's debated issues and close by thinking through what gives a "sure saying" (1 Tim. 1:15; 3:1; 4:9; 2 Tim. 2:11; Titus 3:8) or practice a permanent place in the life of the Church.

Mutable Traditions: Four Cases from Church History

Our first case concerns evangelism and the use of the Old Testament in the apostolic era. At several places in the New Testament, we may discern the apostles' striking use of Isaiah 6 to explain the tragedy of unbelief and the miracle of faith. Not surprisingly, the early Church, in making reference to this dramatic passage, had recourse to the early Septuagint (LXX), the Greek version of the Bible, for that was the text used among Greek-speaking Jews and the growing Christian movement. Isaiah 6:10 is quoted in reference to the mysterious parables (Mark 4:12; Matt. 13:13–16), the blindness of the disciples (Mark 8:17–18), the people's misunderstanding of divine signs or miracles (John 12:40), and the rejection of the gospel by Paul's Jewish brothers (Acts 28:26–27; cf. Rom. 11:8). Here is the verse, translated directly from its LXX wording:

> For the heart of this people has become thick
> And they listen dully with their ears
> And they close their eyes,
> In case they see with their eyes
> And hear with their ears
> And understand with their hearts and turn—
> And I shall heal them. (EH)

This is a troublesome but luminous saying. It begins with the sad situation of a people whose heart, ears, and eyes are impeded so that they cannot receive revelation from God. Indeed, in the context of Isaiah 6, the very preaching of the prophet is *causing* the lack of communication, a shock that is more distinctly registered in the Hebrew rendering of this verse ("*Make* the heart of this people dull . . .") and approximated in John's version ("*He has blinded* their eyes and hardened their heart" [John 12:40a]). In the Greek rendering, followed in Acts and Matthew, the causation is not emphasized but rather the simple fact of the dullness or hard-heartedness of those who do not believe is described. With the exception of Mark, however, all the New Testament citations of Isaiah 6:10 show a clear preference for the surprising more optimistic ending of the verse in question. If the eyes, ears, and heart are not operative, then this means that they cannot hear the message, for if they could, they would turn—and in that case "I *shall* heal them." Both Greek and English speakers naturally anticipate a different ending: the organs are closed "so that they might not hear, see, and understand, and turn, and I *would in that (impossible? unlikely?) case* heal them." Yet the verse, rather ungrammatically, switches from the hypothetical subjunctive mode ("lest"; "in order that they might not"; "in case they might") to the future indicative—"and I shall."

Few translators know what to do with this and simply persist in reproducing in their translation an unlikely possibility. In doing so they miss what appears to capture a more positive vision of God's ability and will to heal. The closing positive future verb seemingly appealed to the evangelists, who, with the exception of Mark, adopt the reading. It was no doubt especially useful to them in demonstrating the miraculous nature of God's power to turn people around and to heal them against all odds and all extenuating circumstances (including a hardened audience). It is particularly odd that John's Gospel, which more closely follows the Hebrew version at the earlier point of the verse, reverts to the LXX ending of hope. Here, the LXX shaped the teaching of the early Church, despite the fact that a Hebrew text of the prophet came earlier—and it looks as though John made a deliberate decision in the closing part of the verse to retain the *second* tradition, the translated Greek tradition, since it corresponded to his understanding that the light shines in the darkness, and illumines it, even where the darkness may not be (at first) willing.

The persistence of this Greek tradition in the translation of Isaiah 6:10 is even more apparent when we consider some of the later versions of Mark 4:12. Here we can see that those who are passing on Mark's Gospel have tried to bring its pessimistic flavor in this case into harmony with the majority New Testament position. A literal translation of the Greek in our earliest manuscripts of Mark 4:12 (and closer to the Hebrew text of Isaiah) is "it *would* be forgiven them," a doubtful hypothetical meaning. Instead, later transmitters in the Western tradition, called the "Bezae Text," conform Jesus' words to Matthew, John, and Acts, and render this as God's will for the future—"I *shall* forgive them."[1] It would seem that those scribes who were passing on this passage were troubled because all the other New Testament versions used the more optimistic future "I shall." Thus, they sought to bring Mark's darker discourse on the parables into conformity with the other passages. To speak of a God who is only hypothetically willing to heal or forgive was not in accord with the apostolic tradition they had received—nor with the gospel story in general.[2] Here, then, we see a surprising insistence of those handling

1. The history of transmission is complex here. B* seems to have altered the subjunctive verb *aphethē*, which signals a hypothetical situation, to *aphthēsomai*, "I shall be put aside, I shall be forgiven," which is future indicative but incoherent since God is not the one to be forgiven. A later revisionist (D2) amends this to *aphēsō*, "I shall put aside, I shall forgive," agreeing with the future indicative but removing the passive so that it makes sense. *Aphēsō* then becomes a synonym for the future verb found in Matthew, Acts, and the LXX—*iasomai* ("I shall heal") but with particular reference to sins being removed. In the view of a renowned specialist, Aland, the Bezae Text may actually be based upon a late third-century papyrus known in the Western church, and so the verse in question may show us a relatively early debate in the Church, not simply a revision that dates to later times such as the sixth to ninth centuries.

2. The question of what Jesus himself actually said, of course, is a complex one. Several options are possible. First, we may speculate that an earlier Hebrew manuscript, unknown to us, contained a more positive reading used by Jesus and that Mark brought the saying into conformity with the Hebrew version that he knew. If this were discovered, it would be delightful for those who prefer the renderings of the later Gospel writers, Matthew and Luke. On the one hand, such a scenario is sheer speculation. On the other hand, scholars who earlier placed the highest value on the Masoretic Hebrew text recently have encountered a few surprises in that newly discovered early Hebrew manuscripts predating the medieval Masoretes

the New Testament to prefer the Greek tradition of Isaiah's wording, even when the Hebrew was known. It was not simply a matter of
preferring the LXX because this was the version honored for a long
time by the early Greek-speaking communities. Rather, in this case the
Greek more readily demonstrated the astonishing clemency of God,
who delights in resurrection and re-creation. Eyes that are blinded,
ears that are stopped, and hearts that are hardened *shall* be healed,
despite the improbability. "Never since the beginning of the world
has it been heard that someone opened the eyes of the blind" (John
9:32 EH)—but that is exactly what Jesus has come to do!

The second case concerns a matter still sometimes debated today,
though mostly in fringe parts of the Church. This is the issue of
"Sabbath keeping," a biblical tradition that is even alluded to in the
first chapter of Genesis, where God "rests" on the seventh day. Sab-
baths are underscored in the giving of the Decalogue, amplified in
Leviticus, underscored in Nehemiah, celebrated in the Psalms, and

---

are, in some few cases, congruent with the LXX version(s) that we possess, rather
than the Masoretic text. Second, it is possible that Jesus did, in the context of his
discussion of the parables, present a grim prophetic picture and entirely meant to
suggest the improbability of his own people's conversion. Third, we might suggest
that he faithfully quoted the pessimistic Hebrew text but with a heuristic purpose
meant to drive the hearers to change, much as the absolute predictive judgments of
the prophets (e.g., Jonah's indictment of Nineveh) were not in fact carried out but
rescinded when the people did repent. In the latter case, which seems most likely to
me, other features of Jesus' teaching would demonstrate that the subjunctive case
used in this prophetic judgment is not the final word: God specializes in resurrection
and so the overall shape of the gospel gives rise to a *future* promise of the triumphant
LORD. The Christian community is, after all, guided by the Scriptures as they have
been received by the Church ("the Holy Spirit will guide you into all truth") and not
by a hypothetical reconstruction of scholars concerning what Jesus originally must
have said. Research concerning the "historical Jesus" is valuable in giving to us a
better historical context for understanding those early years, but its findings should
not displace the Scriptures such as we have received them. All four of the Gospels,
after all, do not give us mere "reportage" of what Jesus said and did (nor is historical reportage without interpretation ever possible). Rather, they relate the actions
and words of Jesus from the perspective of a faith that has been fully rounded by
all the events, including Pentecost and the spread of the gospel to the gentiles. This
is a faith digested and shaped by the living Tradition of the people of God, not a
faith that relies on some static word (always rather elusive) of the LORD. We have
very few of the exact words (*ipsissima verba*) of Jesus, such as *Talitha cum!* (Mark
5:41) and *Amen!* Everywhere in the Gospels, however, we hear his very own voice
(*ipsissima vox*).

viewed with approval by the major prophets.[3] Yet the early Christians relativized the importance of the Sabbath, as we see in Jesus' words and in several of the epistles. The *reasons* for an alteration of the key day from Sabbath to Sunday are fairly straightforward. However, the *continued importance* of the principle, and what it means in practice, continues to divide Christians today: the application is not spelled out carefully in the New Testament writings that document the transition.

Of first importance are Jesus' own words concerning the Sabbath, most notably, "the Son of Man is Lord of the Sabbath" (Mark 2:28 and parallels, EH) and "The Sabbath was not made for humanity, but humanity for the Sabbath" (Mark 2:27 and parallels, EH). These sayings pointedly highlight the specific status of Jesus (who personifies the "Son of Man" of Dan. 7) and the participatory sovereignty of humanity, who is summed up by this lordly "Son of Man": the Sabbath is not intended to be an institution that subjugates but the gift of God. Indeed, this focus upon the root of the Sabbath as a gift rather than a mere obligation is not unique to Jesus, for we find ample evidence in later Jewish literature that the Sabbath was to be a celebratory time, as, for example, in Judith 8:6, where the heroine of that story is commended for *not* fasting on the Sabbath day, the day of joy. Within the context of the Gospels, however, the emphasis takes a surprising turn. Jesus implies that those actions previously considered to break the sanctity of Sabbath do not necessarily do so—he provides food for his disciples, heals, and generally "does good" on the Sabbath, much to the chagrin of those who interpret Torah differently. The Fourth Gospel is even more polemical, where God, whom Genesis tells us rested on the seventh day, is said by Jesus to be the Father who "is always working" (John 5:17 EH)—this warrant gives the Son, his coworker, the same prerogative.

Clearly, the early Christians did not consider that Jesus alone was justified in taking this tack. For although the apostles are described

3. Some Christian readers hold a general view that the prophets did not approve of Sabbath keeping, and so they absolutize such ironic verses as Isa. 1:13 and Amos 8:5, where God seems to scorn this activity. However, the positive (and seemingly eternal) value of Sabbath is underscored in Isa. 56:2, 6; 66:23; Jer. 17:21–27; and Ezek. 46:1. Clearly, the prophetic disapproval of Sabbath celebration concerns hypocrisy, not the practice itself.

in Acts as joining with Jews on the Sabbath for the purposes of proclaiming the good news, there we also hear in passing that the disciples
(customarily?) gathered on the first day of the week (the day of Jesus'
resurrection) to break bread (Acts 20:7), a habit probably confirmed
by St. Paul in 1 Corinthians 16:2 and John the visionary in Revelation
1:10. By the time that the New Testament writings saw the light of day,
Jesus' own habit of going to synagogue on the Sabbath day seems to be
giving way to the custom of meeting for prayer, worship, and the Lord's
Supper on the Lord's Day, the first day of the week. Very soon, if not
at this point, the term "Lord's Day" was to take on a quasi-technical
meaning, for we see it used in the late first and early second century
both in *Didache* 14:1 and in Ignatius' letter to the Magnesians, where
he describes the Christian custom over against Jewish Sabbatarianism.

Surprisingly, the argument between Jewish and gentile believers that
reaches a solution of sorts in Acts 15 makes no mention of Sabbath
keeping, one of the major boundary markers around Judaism along
with circumcision, attention to kosher foods, and the keeping of other
Torah regulations. We know, however, that this was a contentious
issue in the earliest days since Paul alludes to it in Romans 14:5 and
Galatians 4:10, implying that those who are unduly scrupulous about
certain days are "weak" in the faith. This is more pointedly declared
in Colossians 2:16, where Jewish Sabbath observance is classed with
those things that are mere "shadows" of the true substance of the
faith. In a more positive vein, the author of Hebrews tells his readers
that there is indeed a "keeping of Sabbath" sacred to the people of
God (4:9 EH)—that is, the rest of faith in which Christians share,
entering into God's true rest from the dawn of creation. In the words
of the Master: "Something greater . . . is here" (Matt. 12:6, 41, 42).

Early Christians, then, followed the lead of Jesus (as described
in the Gospels) in changing the holy day, for they understood the
resurrection as overriding a custom underscored even in the opening
verses of Torah. Yet it was not simply a matter of transferring strict
Sabbath observance to another day: after all, early Christians would
in most cases have been given no leisure to rest on the Lord's Day, for
Christianity was not licit in those first years. If they did not join with
the Jewish community in Sabbath observance, they would not in most
cases have the opportunity to supplant that day with another like it:

rather, most would have met very early on the Lord's Day to worship, prior to going to work. The "rest" of Sabbath must have been for most of them of the variety described in the letter to the Hebrews—a matter of constant trust in the Lord, recognizing creaturely dependence, and focusing upon the accomplished work of the Son on their behalf. When the Christian faith became legal in the fourth century, Sunday recovered some of the characteristics of the earlier Jewish Sabbath, but the actual extent of the similarities between the two special days continued (and continues) to be debated. St. Paul's letters concerning abstinence from strife among Christians who disagree would continue to have relevance! What we discern from the treatment of the New Testament is, however, that the fate of the Sabbath was bound up closely with that of Torah—Sabbath, the quintessential symbol of Torah, was meant to point to the God of all blessing, creation, and rest. Once the greater has come, the glory of the lesser joy is eclipsed (2 Cor. 3:10–11). The later Christian habit of referring to Sunday as the "eighth day" (rather than the first) implies this logic of fulfillment: what looks like a *change* is rather a surprising outworking of what had been hidden in God's original plan.

In our third case, we move beyond the New Testament to wrestle with why an injunction of the apostolic Church was not kept in perpetuity. At first blush, this is surprising, since the decision is characterized by James as something that seemed "good to the Holy Spirit and to us." The original instruction, documented in Acts 15:20 and 29 (and reiterated in 21:25), placed upon the gentile believers certain mild restrictions concerning food—no eating of food that had been strangled, nor that had not been hung up to remove its blood according to the Torah, nor offered to idols—as well as the avoidance of sexual immorality (*porneia*). The food regulations were given so that table fellowship might be facilitated among gentile believers and Christians who still kept Jewish kosher laws. Our first question is, why was it necessary even to speak about sexual immorality, which is no matter of mere Jewish ceremony but dealt with by Jesus in standards that are higher than those of the Torah? Some have suggested that the reference to *porneia* in Acts 15:29 was a short form for something very specific, that is, to the laws prohibiting marriage within lines of consanguinity (cf. Lev. 18). If this is the case, the original decree may be seen as prohibiting gentile practices concerning food and morality that would have been egregious to Torah-sensitive Christians, smoothing the way for community between these and gentile believers.

As we look at how the manuscripts of Acts 15 were passed down, it becomes apparent that these regulations were eventually considered, by many, no longer to apply to the Church. Why? It may be helpful to note that in Acts 15, when the decision of the council is given down, verbs of commanding are not used, but rather words of opinion and rationalization: "it *seemed* good" and "*for* Moses is read." In the Western text of the New Testament, the rule is rephrased and comes to a conclusion with a negative formulation of the golden rule. Presumably, this gloss on the original text was understood to be its inner meaning—the gentile Christians were originally enjoined *not* to do those things that would be a stumbling block to their Jewish Christian friends, and this is the principle to be held in perpetuity from this moment in Church life. Some Christian communities continued to practice the Acts 15 decision in its particulars: probably this is the case in Revelation 2:14 and 22, as in some second- and third-century Christian communities, and even in evidence as late as ninth-century England.[4] Not all Christians agreed, then, with the reapplication; generally, however, interpreters understood the decree as a compromise decision not intended to be binding for all time. Picking up on the irenic tone of James and the situational character of the decision, they believed that faithfulness to the apostolic word was sufficiently demonstrated by those who kept the spirit, and not the letter, of this decree.

So far we have seen an alteration of tradition on the part of the apostolic community concerning the choice of the Greek over the Hebrew text in the use of Isaiah 6, on the part of New Testament writers in the long-standing custom of keeping Sabbath, and on the part of

4. See the defense of Christians against infanticide by Eusebius in his *Ecclesiastical History* 5.1.26, where he insists that Christians even abstain from the blood of animals. In a similar vein see also Tertullian's *Apology* 9.13 and Justin Martyr's *Dialogue with Trypho* 34.8. The persistence of the tradition is seen also in the preamble to the law code of King Alfred the Great (England, ninth century), who cites Acts 15. The lengthy text of Alfred's introduction is available in F. Liebermann's *Die Gesetze der Angelsachsen* (which I have not seen) and mentioned in Attenborough, *The Laws of the Earliest English Kings*, 34.

the later Church in its application of the apostolic decree of Acts 15. Our final example is a tradition that is more theologically central than these: it concerns the very practice of worship or of prayer and the introduction of a tradition that cannot be found in the Scriptures but that has been practiced widely in the Church, both East and West, for centuries. I refer to the invocation of the Holy Spirit in prayer and the celebration of his[5] name in both personal and formal worship. Quite recently, I was myself challenged by a colleague from a very radical Protestant tradition concerning the practice of the Church in this matter, on the grounds that there is no warrant for it in Scripture, where the pattern is fairly consistent: usually one prays to the Father, or to God, either in or through the Son, or in and through the Holy Spirit (cf. Luke 10:21; Rom. 8:26; 16:27; Gal. 4:6; Col. 3:17). However, since sometimes adoration is offered Jesus (e.g., Rev. 5:9–12) and since there is an example of at least one petitionary prayer offered to Jesus (Acts 7:59), my academic friend was prepared to concede the extension of Christian invocation to the second person of the Trinity. He continued, however, to be unsure about the appropriateness of such traditional prayers as "Come, Holy Spirit" (the Latin hymns *Veni Spiritus Sanctus* and *Veni Spiritus Creator*) or such contemporary songs as "Spirit, we adore you . . ." since these find no parallel in the Scriptures.

Yet we find evidence of the practice of both adoring and invoking the Holy Spirit very early in the history of the Christian community, beginning at least in the second century with Saints Polycarp and Clement of Alexandria who speak of thanks, praise, or glory being given to Father, Son, and Holy Spirit, and St. Hippolytus who refers to "worshipping" the Holy Spirit.[6] Moreover, St. Basil quotes the ancient practice of the Vesperal hymn, which he attributes to the earliest

---

5. I continue to use the masculine pronoun for the Holy Spirit, following the practice of Jesus in the Fourth Gospel, who refers to the Spirit, the Advocate, as *ekeinos* ("that [masculine] one"), despite the neuter grammatical article attached to the Greek *Pneuma* (or the grammatical feminine case of the equivalent Hebrew word, *Ruach*). The personhood of the Holy Spirit is at stake here, as well as the confusion implicit in introducing androgynous metaphors into our picture of God. For further discussion on this, see Humphrey, *Ecstasy and Intimacy*, 23–26, and "Why We Worship God as Father, Son and Holy Spirit."

6. *Martyrdom of Polycarp* 14 and 22, St. Clement of Alexandria's *The Pedagogue* 3.12, and St. Hippolytus' *Against Noetus* 12.5.1.

days of the Church, where praise is given by name to all three persons of the Trinity.[7] Following the same logic used by Larry Hurtado in his defense of belief in the divinity of Jesus in the early Church,[8] the worship practice of Christians is definitive. Adoration and petition of the Holy Spirit was no novelty imported into the Church after the creedal conflict concerning the Trinity had settled in the fourth and fifth centuries. Rather, it is in evidence early and in various locales.

But why did Christians feel free to do this, both informally and in corporate worship, without the pattern being set for them in the New Testament writings? The answer may well be that the pattern *was* set for them by the apostles, and that we simply lack evidence of explicit use until slightly later in the history of the Church—after all, the New Testament was never designed to be a complete code of appropriate conduct and worship but a written witness that summed up the witness of the living apostles to Jesus the Christ. Moreover, the practice of worship given to the Spirit is not at odds with the New Testament writings, who mention the Spirit alongside the Son, who speak consistently in terms of a *personal* Holy Spirit rather than a mere force, who warn strongly (in Jesus' own words) about the danger of blaspheming against the Spirit, and who document the tradition of baptizing "in [or into] the name of the Father and of the Son and of the Holy Spirit" (Matt. 28:19), even though at the beginning (or in some locales) baptism might have been given simply in the name of Jesus (cf. Acts 10:48). If the Spirit is God, and the Spirit is personal, then what would prevent early Christians from offering to the Holy Spirit the same concourse and adoration that they willingly gave Father and Son? Even if the practice of praying to the Spirit took some time to develop, then this seems to be one of those very things about which Jesus said, "The Spirit of truth . . . will guide you into all the truth." Of course, it is normally the delight of the Holy Spirit not to witness to himself but to the Son, whom he teaches us to glorify. Here, then, is a case where a possible *change* in the Holy Tradition was no alteration but rather a deepening of the practice to match the Triune mystery that was being unpacked by God's people. As St. Basil argues to the

7. St. Basil, *On the Holy Spirit* 29.73.
8. Hurtado, *Lord Jesus Christ.*

balkers in his own generation, why should those who know the Holy
Spirit to be God refrain from giving him the praise that is his due?[9]

These four cases of modified tradition are disparate in nature and
in timing, but they have several things in common—all of them are
explicable by close attention to the intent and deeper meaning of the
Scriptures, and by reference to the overall Christian story that finds
its fulfillment in Jesus. The decision to stress the Greek reading of
Isaiah's dark word corresponded to the miracle of repentance and
healing performed by the Son; the decision not to continue a literal
application of Acts 15's decree matched its compromise nature and
a new situation where there was no longer a living dispute between
Torah-observant Jewish and gentile Christians; the practice of allowing work on the Sabbath and honoring the eighth day found deep
resonance in the words of Jesus and in the gospel story, since Jesus'
resurrection had brought new day; and the tradition of praying to
the Holy Spirit was a natural extension of both Jesus' teaching and
the apostolic understanding of who that Spirit really was.

These very "changes" document the living quality of the Church
and help us to see which things remain unchanged and which may
be subject to modification. We may be surprised to see that the Holy
Spirit is not bound to an "original" language of transmission—but
that is in keeping with the astonishing God who can "translate" himself into human form for our sake! We may be concerned that Torah
and Sabbath seem to have been set aside—until we understand that
this was always God's intent, for the Torah and the Sabbath were
both intended to point to Jesus, the Center of all the universe and
the true Promised Rest of God's people. We may at first worry that
if an apostolic council's decisions can be "set aside," then nothing
can stand firm—until we note the signaled intent of that council to
provide a modus operandi for a specific time and place. We may suspect that hymns to the Trinity go beyond what has been given to the
Church—until we take full note of Jesus' teaching concerning that
wonderful Spirit and remember Matthew's witness to Triune baptism,
where there is *one* divine Name that includes the Holy Spirit. It would
appear that of our problem cases, only the case of Acts 15 gives us

9. St. Basil, *On the Holy Spirit* 19, 145.

an example of a true change—and the permission for that mutability is embedded in the apostle James' own signaled intent. In the other three cases, it is not a matter of novelty but of surprising development so that the Tradition is more fully expressed. All four of the cases, moreover, show why it is impossible to detach Scripture from the living Tradition of the Church and pay attention only to the written canon. The question we are driven to ask is, do we trust the words of Jesus who told his disciples that they would be led into all truth?

Debated Traditions Today

With these examples in mind, how might we approach changes in tradition today? Such changes range from cultural issues such as women's attire in worship (head coverings are no longer normally worn), to ecclesial decisions such as celibacy among the clergy, to changes in worship such as modified Trinitarian formulae, to something even as basic as how to approach the reading of Scripture. When evaluating such matters, we do well to understand as fully as possible the reason for the traditions, to determine whether these truly are ancient practices in the Church, and to discern how, or in what manner, they correspond to the faith as a whole.

In terms of head coverings for women, the tradition of reading 1 Corinthians 11:2–19 literally has been long-standing in the Christian tradition, yet most today dismiss the practice as only having a cultural importance. From one perspective, the contemporary decision not to cover may be justified, since St. Paul himself offers cultural reasons for his judgment in verses 6, 13, and 16, when he mentions the first-century appearance of bare-headed prostitutes, the necessity to "judge" for ourselves, and the fact that this is simply a common practice of the churches as a whole. We might notice, however, that the apostle also appeals to theological principles such as the headship of the Father over the Son (11:3) and refers to cosmic mysteries, such as the angels (11:10) who lead worship (Rev. 4–5) and who are themselves known to "cover" as they worship (Isa. 6:2). In a twenty-first-century context, where hats are not normally worn indoors by women except for decorative purposes, the revitalization of this practice might well defeat the apostle's main purpose—to remove distraction so that worship can be about God and not about human (or female) glory. On the other hand, there are some Christian communities that continue this practice as a witness to the beauty of humility, where covered women continue to remind the entire worshiping body of the wonder that all have been called into the presence of a holy God. Those who maintain the practice are well advised to remember theological reasons for their action and avoid mere antiquarianism or a fixation on "proper conduct" at all costs; the practice should not impede their ability to reach out to an unchurched generation that knows nothing of these matters. On the other hand, the majority of women who have dropped the tradition will do well to avoid arrogance in their new "freedom" and should neither belittle nor dismiss those who continue the tradition or their ancestors who embodied it in all piety. Where the practice itself is deemed archaic, there is still a need to remember and hold to the theological, doxological, and practical reasons for St. Paul's injunctions: this will mean finding new ways to express reverence, to concentrate upon God, and to acknowledge the complex interplay between male and female in a day that has forgotten such mysteries.

What to say about celibacy? It is probably unwise to raise this contentious issue at the very end of a discussion on tradition, given the knee-jerk reaction against celibacy of the clergy that is being seen in many Christian quarters today—an understandable reaction to sexual misconduct coming to light in the Church. Many concerned and compassionate laypersons have strong feelings about the issue, assuming that their leaders would not have engaged in such appalling behavior had they not been driven to it by deprivation. In contrast, twenty-first-century single Christians committed to chastity will surely acknowledge the marginalized position in which they find themselves in a society that is so saturated with sex and that even presumes full humanity cannot be experienced without sexual or physically erotic expression.[10] This ought not to be the experience of Christians in any age, for Jesus in the Gospels (Matt. 19:10) and St. Paul in the letters

10. The definition of "sexual" is a tricky matter, and most psychologists would say that we are sexual beings even when we do not engage in erotic behavior. I am speaking specifically of the action and the desire or energy that fuels erotic actions. It is assumed by many today that this natural part of human experience is necessary

(1 Cor. 7:38) hold forth the life of celibacy as an appropriate expression of devotion to God and as a gift to the Church. However, true celibacy (and even chastity) are so misunderstood today that these verses are either ignored or put down to antiquated disapproval of sex that we have overcome in our more psychologically sound day.

Several things are to be noticed here. The first is that in the original experience of the Church, pastors were not required to be celibate. Indeed there were even "some voices who read into the 'husband of one wife' phrase in the pastoral letters an obligation for bishops (clerics) to be married . . . [because] a cleric ought to have proved his worth in the married state."[11] There was, of course, a general high regard in the early Church for celibacy. Despite this, many took note of the marital status of St. Peter (who had a mother-in-law), and they continued to resist (especially in the East) the intermittent attempts to require celibacy of clergy.[12] In the West, the necessity for upper levels of clerics to be unmarried became a part of canon law; this was not entirely the case in the East. Rather, the Eastern Church found it expedient to select its bishops from the ranks of either widows or unmarried monks, since such men exemplified holiness and a man unencumbered with a family was freer to circulate among far-flung geographical areas, moving from parish to parish as he exercised his ministry. This pattern became canon law at the Sixth Ecumenical Council (honored by both East and West), which upholds the ideal of celibacy for leaders of the Church on the grounds of the intrinsic good of celibacy, the avoidance of scandal, the unhappy practice of some bishops attempting to pass on the episcopacy to sons, and the impracticality of the episcopate for a married bishop who has household concerns. This canon has been applied rigorously to the episcopate in both the East and the West and also almost without exception to priests in the Western churches.

---

for a fully fulfilled life. The Christian tradition, while at its best affirming erotic drives and actions within marriage, has said otherwise.

11. Heid, *Celibacy in the Early Church*, 172.

12. Especially notable in this regard is St. Chrysostom, who continued to champion the cause of married clergy, including bishops, as is seen in his homilies on 1 Timothy. It should be mentioned, however, that the ascetic ideal was very strong even in the East, so that frequently the wives of married men who became bishops entered monasteries, freeing their husbands to exercise their episcopal ministry in a state of celibacy.

Celibacy for the upper clergy, then, has a long and august history, though the debate continues as to whether it is merely a matter
of expedient tradition or immutable Holy Tradition into which the
Church has been led. This is not the place to weigh in on the matter,
since my own scholarly opinion is of far less value than the decision
of the entire Church. Nevertheless, I would suggest that clarity and
charity are both enjoined upon those concerned for this feature of
ecclesial life. Clarity requires us to acknowledge that celibacy is given a
special place of honor in the Church's life, while marriage is not to be
despised. Clarity also requires us to note that canon laws concerning
the celibacy of bishops (and in the West, priests) were enacted not
only to exalt celibacy but also because of the situation of the times
and out of consideration for what is "helpful" to the Church. Those
who continue to uphold this ideal must do so without distorting
the reasons for the Church's opinion and without elevating Tradition (or tradition) in this case to the rank of foundational doctrine.
Those who believe that the canons were mostly enacted for the sake
of expediency, and that they therefore may faithfully, at some point,
be repealed, ought to remember the Tradition of celibacy as a gift of
the Spirit: this perspective will entail avoiding uncharitable arrogance
and not despising the practice as it unfolded in the Church. It may
well be that the faithful presence of celibate leaders is a significant
witness to an age that tends to idolize sexual expression. Those who
believe that the Spirit has led the Church into an ideal situation need
to remember the particular burden born by their celibate leadership
and not look down on those parts of the Church that practice differently. Patience, charity, and clarity should guide our thinking and
discussion of these matters.[13]

13. Though a good deal more is at stake theologically in the present discussion
concerning the ministry of women in the Church, these principles hold good in this
issue as well. Far more heat than light often may be discerned in these discussions,
which should be guided by careful attention to the history of the Church (as well as
to the theological foundations of the Tradition) and by careful love and generosity of
spirit toward those with whom we disagree. In another connected matter, we might
consider the prime bone of contention of Orthodox and Protestants with Catholics—the claims of the papacy to universal jurisdiction. Though as an Orthodox I
believe that the papal claims are exaggerated (though a certain primacy of Peter must
be historically acknowledged), I do not myself think that this is the age in which a

Our third example goes to the very center of the Church's theological teaching. I refer to the growing practice of altering the Triune name of God in the light of contemporary concerns for inclusivity. In the case of this change in the Tradition of the Church (a tradition that goes back to the closing verses of Matthew) it seems clear that we are dealing with an unwarranted modification of an immutable truth. Of course, the Church has inherited different ways of speaking about the Holy Trinity, not simply Father, Son, and Holy Spirit ("Holy God, Holy Mighty, Holy Immortal!"), but these extra formulations have always assumed that the baptismal Name is implied. Moreover, attention to the theological reasons given for this change shows the radical nature of the change. Those who put forward alternate formulae such as "Creator, Sustainer, Redeemer," "Rock, Redeemer, Friend," or even "Mother, Child, and Womb," do so on the basis of "metaphorical theology"—an approach that declares all words to be relative to human understanding, including the traditional Name for the One whom we worship. In this account of Christian theology, all words are seen as mere approximations to an ineffable mystery about God, and so "many names" are helpful (and necessary) as human beings reach into their thesaurus of experience to try to address a fundamentally unknown God. Like all plausible arguments, this one is a half-truth. It is indeed the case that God in his essence is unknown. Yet the gospel declares that this One has been known to us truly, if not exhaustively, in Jesus the Son, incarnate for our sake, and through the Holy Spirit. Moreover, the God-Man has taken upon his lips our own feeble human words and directed our speech, revealing to us that "Abba Father, Son, and Holy Spirit" are true names. We have here not simply a theological formula, but the family name revealed by Jesus and received by the apostles. Any relativizing of the Name is a foundational departure from the faith and a break with the faithful family that has preceded us.

---

formal repudiation of this would be of help to the Roman Catholic communion. The many changes since Vatican II and the crisis of the authority in that communion have rendered it so fragile that without the traditional respect offered to the pontiff, many of the good things associated with that communion (its pro-life stance, its holding to the holy mysteries, its traditions of prayer and creed) might well disintegrate as well. A formal repudiation of the doctrine of papal infallibility would certainly smooth the way for reconciliation—but would there be a recognizable Catholic community with which to reconcile, were this action to be taken at this time?

This is not simply a theological nicety, but a debate that has real and serious consequences in the Church. Can the historic Church recognize the baptism of a child (or adult) that has been done under one of the alternate "names"? And it is not merely a matter of form. Can those who are considering these cases (becoming more and more common) be certain that the baptism was performed with the intent of joining this person to the God worshiped by the Christian family? Or was the baptism into an unknown god whose character alters according to the scruples of those who feel they are not included or according to the changing fashions of scholars and liturgists? Among those congregations and communities that continue to use the Name formally in baptisms or in benedictions, what does it mean that "Father, Son, and Holy Spirit" is less and less invoked in these services—does not the continual cry of God's people shape us into what we are meant to be? The naming of God is no mere academic matter nor a matter of historic human tradition. Rather, it is the summary of the entire gospel, the name that gives us identity and the bedrock upon which we give glory to the Holy One. As St. Paul puts it, "Because you are sons, God has sent the Spirit of his Son into our hearts, crying, 'Abba! Father!'" (Gal. 4:6). Here, then, is a clear Tradition of the Church that cannot be altered without distorting our common life. We must find a different way to address the concerns of twenty-first-century women whose experience of a human father is painful and who mistakenly believe that masculine language for God marginalizes them in the community.

Our final example is conceptually linked to the previous one. A whole generation of Christians (in Protestant and Catholic churches alike) is now being raised by hearing versions of the Psalms that are systematically neutralized for gender.[14] The pastoral reasons for this are obvious; however, sometimes there have been unforeseen theological implications. For example, Psalm 1, which in the original states explicitly "Blessed is the *man*" (Hebrew, *ish* not *adam*; Greek, *anēr* not *anthropos*), is rendered in the plural "Blessed are those" in order

---

14. Among Protestants, the inclusive language extends often to references to God; the American Roman Catholic Church uses an altered version of the New American Bible, which reverts to masculine language for God but retains inclusive language in reference to human beings.

to facilitate its appropriation by women alongside men. In making this move, translators have unwittingly obscured an age-old tradition in the Church that leads us to read the Psalms christologically. This practice has been obscured for a very long time in Protestant churches, which have promoted a more psychological reading of the Psalter, pointing to its remarkable capacity to encapsulate every aspect of human emotion and experience. While the Psalter is astonishingly helpful in expressing human emotion, it does not always match our experience but finds its historic context in the life of Israel. The psalms of imprecation (calling down judgment upon enemies) have often been encountered as stumbling blocks by those who assume that the main purpose of the Psalms is to express a Christian mind-set and emotive reaction to experiences of life.

There are many competent and faithful Christians who can help the believing community to understand these difficulties.[15] However, I want to reflect most particularly on the loss of a traditional approach to the Psalms that struck me forcibly when I first attended Great Vespers in the Eastern tradition. At the point when the first Psalm "Blessed is the man" was recited, the priest moved physically to stand before the icon of Christ on the right of the doors to the sanctuary. As we sang, he embodied our meditation upon that only One who is so blessed, that only One who "walks not in the counsel of the ungodly," that only One who in every way is a "tree that yields fruit" and who in all his ways prospers. No one needed to explain the her-meneutical key to me—it was traced in the actions of the liturgy, and I was greatly amazed. On returning home, I remembered all the other Psalms that the evangelists understood to illumine Christ, in particular the heartbreaking Psalm 22 (21 LXX), which ends so triumphantly. And I started to think about the fact that this tradition of reading, so Luke tells us, began with Jesus himself, who showed the two on the road to Emmaus that Moses, the prophets, and "all the Scriptures" pointed to him. Jesus even had used this strategy in debating with the Pharisees who would not recognize his sovereignty; citing Psalm 110:1 (109:1 LXX), he intimated that the Messiah is not, in the final analysis, David's *son* but David's *Lord* (Luke 20:41–42)! But many

---

15. Among many other helpful volumes, see C. S. Lewis's *Reflections on the Psalms*.

Christians have all but lost this approach to the Psalter, reading it less frequently and usually with an eye to existential expression of their own emotions. In abandoning this apostolic hermeneutic, Christians have lost a key connection with that living Tradition that reads the written Word in connection with the One who is the Word.[16] What appears to be simply a cosmetic alteration for the sake of more easy appropriation—a change in translation from singular to plural—is bound up with an erosion of the principle of the "rule of faith," which we will discuss more thoroughly in the conclusion to this book.

Which Saying Is Sure?

We have seen, then, several examples of changes in tradition in the history of the Church and in contemporary practice—some of them more marginal in terms of theological significance, others very central indeed. We have noted that it is not easy to distinguish, merely on the basis of whether the matter is mainly theological or cultural, between what is *a* tradition, and therefore potentially subject to change, and what is part of the Holy Tradition. While worship of the Holy Spirit is almost exclusively a theological matter, the other debated items we have considered are disparate in nature and linked to cultural concerns.

There is an intriguing phenomenon in the Pastoral Letters that should warn us against deciding that something is not part of Tradition because it does not appear to be "purely theological." This is the little refrain "this saying is sure and worthy of all acceptance." This formal assurance is found attached not only to central Christian doctrine such as the atonement (1 Tim. 1:15), the utter faithfulness of God (2 Tim. 2:11–13), and justification (Titus 3:8), but also in relation to the office of bishop (1 Tim. 3:1) and the value of godliness over bodily training (1 Tim. 4:8). Practical matters, then, can be part of the solemnly passed-on and carefully received living Tradition of the Church. Perhaps the one clear indication of the presence of the living Tradition is its integral *connection* with Christian story or

16. For help in recovery of this approach, readers may find very useful the careful and illuminating work of Fr. Patrick Henry Reardon, *Christ in the Psalms.*

with revelation about the Triune God as passed down to us by the apostles: Would a change to this custom do damage to the gospel or to our understanding of God? The discernment as to whether a particular practice has this integral link to the deposit of faith is sometimes immediately apparent. More often, however, this is a discernment not to be made quickly and/or in solo by theologian, scholar, liturgist, or even a community: patience and attention to the entire witness of the Church are indicated. Such characteristics do not come easily even to the Church in our restless and quickly paced age. The coming-to-age of the doctrine of the Trinity and overt worship given to the Holy Spirit should be a sign to us against arrogance or impatience. In time, the apostolic decree of Acts 15 was found to be extraneous to the ongoing Tradition, since its motivation was mainly utilitarian and the context had changed. Whenever such a decision is made, however, the attitude with which we treat earlier decisions of the Church matters. Just because a tradition is no longer helpful in carrying the Tradition does not mean that we should look down upon those who came before us. Not all human traditions or culturally specific decisions are death dealing, and many have served their purposes well in past generations. Patience and regard for the whole Church, charity and clarity, love and truth, must meet together as we consider and debate such matters.

CONCLUSION

The Rule of Faith

If we were to say, "All that happened in the Christian past does not represent anything great, anything new; all that was nothing but an aberration and not worth the historian's sympathetic curiosity nor any effort to rediscover its essential vitality," then we would be making a false historical judgment and this would cause harm to the maintenance and renewal of Christian culture . . .

We would be making just as serious an error . . . if we admired the ancient constructs so much that we longed to make them our permanent dwelling . . . or if we believed that fidelity to an author meant copying him or imitating him down to the very letter. . . . This would be to emigrate from the present world without being able to find a homeland in the past.[1]

This judgment is found in the first chapter of Fr. Henri de Lubac's monumental book on *Scripture in the Tradition*. Stated baldly without its surrounding context, the statements may perhaps be misleading—indeed the author concedes that he is exaggerating in order to make a point. Moreover, he is not speaking generally about Christian doctrine but specifically about ways of reading the Scriptures. His purpose is to lay the groundwork for a careful discussion of the

---

1. De Lubac, *L'Écriture dans la tradition*, 12–13. The translation is my own.

way(s) in which the Scriptures have been interpreted in the Christian tradition, and especially to provide a foundation upon which the allegorical and typological approach of the fathers can be authentically appropriated today, without abandoning our concerns for genre and historical query—indeed, as he points out, ancient and contemporary approaches need not be mutually exclusive.

Our main quest in this study has been to examine the theme of tradition in the Scriptures, rather than Scripture as read by the Tradition. At every point, however, these two concerns are linked, since Scripture is enveloped by Tradition and Tradition is enshrined in Scripture. De Lubac's judgment reminds us of what we observed in the last chapter, that some traditions are ephemeral, yet still there is a "constant"[2] or unbroken Tradition that includes perceiving the Scriptures with what he calls "spiritual intelligence."[3]

A colorful illustration used by second-century St. Irenaeus is helpful in showing us how important it is to read the Scriptures in continuity with the whole of God's people and why the interpretation of the Scriptures, in light of that Tradition, is an inside activity for the Christian family more akin to art than to science. In the first section of his argument *Against Heresies*, Irenaeus suggests that we think in these terms: someone is manhandling the mosaic representation of a king that has been formed from precious jewels and is moving around the pieces to make instead the shape of a dog or fox. The portrait of the animal is made from the same materials as the original one, but a picture of an animal is not the same as that first picture. Similarly, it is possible to take all the elements of the Scriptures (and also of Tradition) but to so deform them that another thing entirely emerges. This is the method, charges Irenaeus, of the Gnostic group known as the Valentinians, whom he describes as rewriting and deforming what they have received in order to create and pass on something entirely different. Of course, because the pieces of stone were originally shaped and cut for the portrait of the king, those who try to make out a fox or dog are working against the grain and so they must force the pieces, ending up inevitably with pieces that will not fit and with

2. Ibid., 40.
3. The title of his first chapter is "L'Intelligence spirituelle."

disagreements among themselves. The internal and external lack of coherence is an indication that something is not right. Indeed, their primary sources are not really the Scriptures, nor will they listen to correction from the oral witness of the apostles. Instead, foundational to their new creation is another system of secret knowledge into which they are determined to squeeze (or artificially extend) the biblical passages. Their system was not learned from the Lord or the prophets[4] but is rather a novelty based upon the ideas that matter is inherently opposed to spirit and that human beings are, in essence, divided into three separate groups,[5] each with different ability to grasp the "truth."

It is St. Irenaeus' presupposition that there is a way to understand Scriptures deriving from the apostles (and so from the Lord) that captures our attention. An approach is, by nature, something that is best taught personally and not on paper—as a young pianist learns when trying to "weight" her finger to produce the same rich tone as her teacher. Learning such techniques from a book is nearly impossible. St. Irenaeus, writing in a day before the ecumenical creeds were formally established by councils, was well aware of the personal and oral/aural dimensions of Christian tradition. In a subsequent paragraph of the *Against Heresies* beyond the one we have considered, he spoke of the importance of the "canon of truth" (*kanōn tēs alētheias*),[6] a concept found also in the West, which used the phrase *regula fidei*, or "rule of faith." Because the words "canon" and "rule" are used to articulate this concept, many have assumed that the ancients used the term to indicate a list of holy books or a statement of faith that was a precursor to the creeds. It is certainly the case that the Old Testament Scriptures were honored, that some of the memoirs and letters of the apostles were solemnly heeded, and that there were certain recited paragraphs that summed up the faith at this time. Irenaeus and others who spoke of the "rule" or "canon" seem to have something broader in view. For Irenaeus describes the canon of truth as something that helps Christians to discern that the fox is not the same as the king. It is an arbiter or measuring stick given to them internally in baptism and shared

4. All the above description comes from St. Irenaeus, *Against Heresies* 1.8.1.
5. St. Irenaeus, *Against Heresies* 1.7.5.
6. St. Irenaeus, *Against Heresies* 1.9.4.

with the whole faithful community, enabling them to discern where
the sayings, parables, and parts of Scripture fit with the whole of the
body of truth. Indeed, for the sake of argument, he declares that there
are Christians who have no direct recourse to the Scriptures (for they
cannot read) but who keep in their heart the ancient tradition of the
apostles, including its teachings about the true God, Jesus, the hope of
glory, and adherence to a way of life in continuity with the apostles.
Such barbarians, he argues, would easily recognize and reject heresy,
for they have joined themselves to the Church, even though they do
not know the Scriptures in an immediate way![7]

The discernment comes, then, through the believer's incorporation into the body of Christ, and it includes a way of reading the
Scriptures that illumines Christ. Other early fathers such as Justin
Martyr insisted that the Scriptures needed to be rightly interpreted,
since even the prophets speak about those who can read their words
with "no understanding."[8] Moreover, it would seem that this right
handling of Scripture is found only where true teaching, traditions,
and faith are also found.[9] St. Cyril of Jerusalem reminds those who
are preparing for baptism that the creed they are to memorize was
not based on human opinion, but that it is a summary of something
more foundational, collected out of all of Scripture, and conform-
ing to the traditions of the apostles that embraced both the Old and
New Testaments.[10] We are reminded of the impulse of the evangelist
Matthew, who describes a scribe trained for the kingdom of heaven
as "a householder who brings out of his storehouse things that are
new and old" (Matt. 13:52 EH). This appropriate bringing out of the
storehouse depends upon the rule of faith. For all these early theologians, Scriptures (beginning with the Old Testament) are understood
to be the written and concrete core of Holy Tradition, only fully
understandable within the context of the Church, which reads them
in light of the rule of faith passed down from the apostles. The canon
or rule is, as it were, the lens by which the Scriptures come into focus
and by which the Tradition is authentically transmitted.

7. St. Irenaeus, *Against Heresies* 3.4.1–2.
8. Justin Martyr, *Dialogue with Trypho* 70.
9. Tertullian, *On the Prescription of Heresies* 15.19.
10. St. Cyril of Jerusalem, *Catechetical Lectures* 5.12.

Reading with the Fathers

Fr. John Breck discerns eight principles in the way that the Church fathers read the holy books—and probably by which they made later decisions concerning those books labeled "canonical," that is, embodying the canon of truth. These principles demonstrate that fruitful biblical interpretation is "a function of the liturgical life of the Church"[11] rather than something undertaken in the study by the isolated scholar applying his or her own methods to traditional materials. Attention to these principles will ensure that those today who interpret the Scriptures continue to lift up the "doxological" quality of the Scriptures and will encourage them to acknowledge their own role as servants, or deacons, of the people of God. Here are the principles, rephrased for brevity:[12]

1. The Word of God refers in the first place to the Son, the personal Logos.
2. True reading of Scripture requires a Trinitarian perspective.
3. Scripture is theandric ["theanthropic"?], both divine *and* human.
4. Interpretation of Scripture is to help the Church and for salvation.
5. New Testament writings are the norm for the whole Tradition.
6. The Old and New Testaments are related as promise and fulfillment.
7. Scriptural passages should be interpreted by reference one to the other.
8. Scripture must be interpreted within a life of prayer and commitment.

The implications of these principles, drawn from the early fathers, serve as an apt summary to what we have explored in this study. The first four principles concern the character of the Scriptures seen in the light of the gospel narrative. First, the written Word is not an end in itself but points to the One who is the Word—Christians are first of all "Christ's ones," and because of that they are "People of the Book." Second, though it took ages for the mystery of the Trinity to

11. Breck, *Scripture in Tradition*, 44.
12. Ibid., 45–46.

be revealed, the Scriptures come to us from that One who is the Father of our Lord Jesus Christ, who by his Word created the world and by his Spirit sustains and renews it. Third, just as Jesus is the God-Man, so too in Scriptures we hear both the divine Voice and human voices: there is a correlation between the divine Word and the written Word. Often in the Scriptures these voices speak in unison or harmony, and sometimes, it seems, the human voice is only transiently or partially true, so that it must be corrected or modified at subsequent parts of the revelatory text. Scripture is not simply for the purposes of aesthetics (though there are some beautiful passages) nor in order to teach us history (though it gives us a window into other human cultures) nor to give special esoteric knowledge (though sometimes we have glimpses of the unseen): ultimately these things are written "that you might believe . . . and have life" (John 20:31 EH).

Principles five through seven concern interrelationships between the various "parts" of God's revelation. When we acknowledge the New Testament as the norm, we recognize that it is the climax of God's revelation, the culmination of the story of Adam and Israel. Further, we acknowledge that it is through this concrete expression of the New Testament that the ancient theologians resolved their debates concerning the mysteries of Christology, the Holy Trinity, and the nature of the Church. Where there is a flat contradiction of a tradition by the whole Scriptures, something is wrong. In order to understand the "whole Scriptures," however, the relationship between Old and New must be probed: they are linked together as promise and fulfillment, as we see in the brief description of Jesus' words on the road to Emmaus and in the method of the Gospel writers (especially Matthew, who makes this explicit in his formulaic refrain, "that the Scriptures [or prophets] . . . might be fulfilled" [Matt. 26:56, cf. Matt. 2:17, 23; 4:14; 13:14; 26:54; 27:9]).

In the last of this trio of principles, we are told that various parts of Scripture are mutually illuminating. This is the principle of "exegetical reciprocity"[13] that we noted in chapter 2 of this study during our analysis of rabbinic and early Church methods of interpretation. For Christians who acknowledge the inherent unity of the Bible, this

13. Ibid., 46.

should not be particularly disturbing, especially when we use chronologically later passages in order to clarify ones written earlier: as the
traditional saying goes, "The Old Testament is in the New revealed."
However, when the lines of reciprocity go the other way (that is, where
"the New Testament is in the Old concealed"), this can be a challenge
for the twenty-first-century mind-set. The historian is correct not to
use this principle anachronistically, for example, and will refrain from
declaring that Daniel *knew* the young men were encountering Jesus
when he saw one "like a son of man" (7:13) in the fiery furnace with
them. However, when the interpreter is clear about the task, separating
out historical intent on the part of the human authors from thematic
or figurative analysis done in a more traditional mode, then no damage
is done. Obscure passages may be clarified by means of those that are
clearer. More daringly, events or figures that have a specific historic
meaning in the Old Testament may be linked, in the light of the rule
of faith, with the New. This is both a New Testament and patristic
principle. For Paul, the obedience of Abraham points forward to the
Christian obedience of faith; in ancient hymnody, the burning bush
that is not consumed is a sign pointing forward to the mother of God
the Son, who bore within her human body complete divinity.

The final statement in Fr. Breck's summary moves us beyond both
the realms of exegesis (that is, the explanation of the words of the text)
and interpretation (the explanation of its implications in the light of a
larger theology) to transformation. It reminds us that if in the Scriptures
we meet the One who is the Light, we must expect to be changed. The
ancient rabbis, before and after handling the sacred words, washed their
hands. Those of us who read Scriptures likewise do best to remember
that we are handling holy things: prayer and life in the Church is the
sine qua non for faithful reading, and faithful reading will inform our
prayers and the life of the Church. Most recently Fr. Theodore Stylianopoulos, adding to the historical, literary, and theological dimensions
of Scripture observed by Bishop N. T. Wright, has insisted that we
must note also the ultimate dimension of *theoria* or transformation.[14]

To be sure, we need to understand all these principles in the light
of how the ancient theologians actually worked, and in reading the

14. Stylianopoulos, *The New Testament*, 1:215–16.

fathers we will notice that, from time to time, they did not always adhere to these principles. After all, each generation has its blind spots, and we need each other, through the ages, for complete understanding. Sometimes, in observing interpreters from times past, we will be disturbed to see them leave behind the literal meaning of the text entirely, forgetting that the historical is the arena in which God works in order to draw us to himself: over against this slip, the fathers, at their most perceptive, insisted that the deeper meaning of the text was not meant to overrule the first and most natural literal meaning. Especially helpful for today will be a robust recovery of that method used by St. Paul and the fathers, whereby we see in the Old Testament events and persons that direct us to Christ—both by means of contrast and by means of fulfillment. This method, we are reminded by Fr. Breck, was "passed on from apostolic times through the entire patristic period"[15] and is not hostile to a historical reading of historical material. Rather, careful typological insight shows us how God uses his creation to illumine us, to lead us to *theoria*, or what de Lubac calls "spiritual intelligence." To recover this method is not to regress, nor should we conflate or confuse this kind of reading with the critical methods—it is not as though the human author of Genesis had knowledge of the Holy Trinity and the incarnate Word. But if Genesis is theanthropic (having both a divine and human element), then the Holy Spirit can lead us to ask questions not only about authorial intent and original cultural context but also about the deeper truth and the One who is Truth, to which and to whom these things point. From this perspective, the Word was present with the Father, cocreating, when God *said* "Let there be light" (cf. John 1:1), and the Spirit was there too, brooding over the waters and especially when God deliberated, "Let *us* make Adam."

Toward the Great Tradition

More than five years ago, North Park University scholar Bradley Nassif documented the renewed interest in the Christian "Great Tradition."

15. Breck, *Scripture in Tradition*, 50.

Of course, the term has been borrowed from literary and historical studies, where it originally referred to the classical authors and elements that have shaped, for example, our Western world. Applied to the Church, "Great Tradition" comes to mean "the theological consensus of the first 500 to 1,000 years of Christian history [that] encompasses the Church's universally agreed upon creeds, councils, fathers, worship, and spirituality."[16] His article stresses the fascination of many in the Western Church with a classical Christianity that integrated its reading and understanding of Scripture with a sense of historic continuity.

The "Great Tradition" that was established in those formative centuries (or first millennium) did not, of course, preclude human sin and confusion—the strength of the Gnostic movement, the Arian conflict, and garden-variety scandals in those years make this clear. Nevertheless, that Tradition has been transmitted in clear and unmistakable ways: through the complex fourfold refraction of the Gospels; through assurance concerning the resurrection by eyewitnesses of various kinds; through baptism by which we are joined together in the Church and given the water of the Holy Spirit; through the traditions in the New Testament and the historic liturgies concerning the Eucharist; through painful yet truthful accounts of the debates in the Church from the earliest times (and how these were resolved); and through the life of Christians, diverse in expression yet continuing to show forth, in contrast with the world around, the wonder of transformation in Christ. The Great Tradition, then, encompasses not simply the transmission of the gospel in narrative form and doctrine in terms of creedal propositions but also a common approach to morals, life habits, and shared worship that connects Christians together across time and centuries.

The first century epistle of Jude, in reflecting upon the first installment of this rich deposit, speaks about our "common salvation, . . . the faith that was once for all handed down to the holy ones" (Jude 3 EH). Despite the security afforded this treasure because it was held in common, and despite his assurance that the faith had been enacted in a once-for-all manner, that first-century author was compelled to write

16. Nassif, "Will the 21st Be the Orthodox Century?"

about the faith yet again, contending for it as something that had to
be carefully maintained. An astonishing gift has been bequeathed by
means of the Incarnate One, who abides still with his Church through
the indwelling Holy Spirit. This is a gift that is complete, delivered
from Jesus to the apostles and so to us. Yet it is a gift that is held in
the hope of his return and that presently bears fruit, sending up shoots
that are living and health-giving in changed circumstances and among
communities that speak different languages. Just as it is not enough
to know a summary of the fathers' methods distilled into principles
(but one must read the ancient theologians for oneself),[17] so it is not
enough merely to acknowledge the various expressions of the Great
Tradition and to look for the imprint of these upon our own faith
communities. Rather, to dwell consciously within the living Church
is to move beyond an appreciative interest in the Great Tradition to
see that it abides today in an undying and vital Holy Tradition bequeathed to the Church, whom Jesus promised would be led into all
truth. It is, then, to *inhabit* the Tradition: to recite the creeds with
joy and in harmony with the entire Church, to enter into devotional
writings such as the *Philokalia*, and to worship by means of ancient
hymns and liturgies and by means of actions, prayers, and music fully
informed by that same life.

A fruitful understanding of Holy Tradition, then, will mean going
beyond a mere antiquarian curiosity about the past and even beyond a
novice's fascination with what seem to be esoteric Christian traditions.
Indeed, the actions of some contemporary Christians who are meeting
part of the Tradition for the first time and want, with all good intent,
to incorporate them into their own personal and congregational life,

17. For those to whom the ancient theologians of the Church are relatively unknown, I recommend beginning with the Ancient Christian Commentary on Scriptures
series (InterVarsity). This is, however, simply a beginning, since the method pursued in
these volumes is to print helpful but relatively short selections of key Church fathers
after the pertinent sections of the biblical text. The coordinates for these selections are
offered, however, and from this beginning, the novice can move on to the actual texts
themselves, available in the original and almost always in multiple English translations.
Translations most readily available on the internet (e.g., at http://www.newadvent.org
/fathers) are not the most recent and therefore sometimes contain stilted English (at
least to our twenty-first-century ears); however, they are drawn from what have been
the standard translations for over a century. Those for whom style matters more would
be advised to taste some of the newer translations that are being published today.

may be too hasty. Without careful reflection, the newcomer risks a mere "cherry-picking" of the Tradition, so that he or she acts without a full understanding of how the practice that is so alluring might actually contradict his or her own (and more local) tradition and theology. Rather than an edifice with firm foundations, the result might be instead a strange and cobbled-together expression of the faith, devoid of natural growth and fluidity, and more akin to a child's rickety tree house that has been constructed out of whatever has come to hand. It is a curious thing, for example, to see Reformed Christians worshiping with icons when they have not gone back to reconsider the implications of these, given their own strong iconoclastic ("icon-smashing") tradition. Even more curious is the phenomenon of the Anglican Church of Canada's *Book of Alternative Services*, which, with all good intentions, has omitted the *filioque* from its contemporary service but retained it in the traditional one, as though the centuries-old debate between East and West were merely a matter of taste![18]

18. *Book of Alternative Services*. The contemporary service of "The Holy Eucharist" omits the phrase "from the Son" (Latin, *filioque*) in the confession of the Holy Spirit (p. 189), whereas "The Holy Eucharist: A Form in the Language of the Book of Common Prayer 1962" has reformulated the structure of the Eucharist according to the precepts of the liturgical renewal movement but retains ancient forms including the phrase "Who proceeds from the Father *and the Son*" (p. 234). In the first case, the creed is altered from the usual Anglican usage in order to accord with the early form of the historic creed, whereas in the second case the creed is printed according to the Western tradition, handed down by the Roman Church after the eighth century. It is clear that those who compiled the new book of services had been impressed by the ecumenical *Baptism, Eucharist and Ministry* discussions and were intent to move the Canadian Anglican Church toward a form of recitation that was charitable to the East and open to ecumenical action. However, no decision was made with regard to the *theology* of this alteration (or the editors would not have included the earlier formula in the more traditional service), nor was any teaching done in the Canadian Anglican churches who have, for the most part, adopted the *Book of Alternative Services* contemporary service as a new standard in practice. It is insufficient to assume that theology is insignificant in making such an alteration and that the change should be made simply because this was, historically, the earliest form of the creed, before the *filioque* was unilaterally imposed by the papacy upon the West. After all, this was a major catalyst for the Great Schism, and the argument at that time did not simply concern authority (though it included this): it was also a matter of theological substance. I would be happy to hear Canadian Anglicans reciting the original form of the creed if I were convinced that they knew why they were doing it. To see that the most commonly used book of services in Canada has two renderings, offered in tandem at 8:00 a.m. followed by 11:00 a.m. without explanation, does not give that confidence.

Coming to grips with the Great Tradition, and with the idea of Holy Tradition over against mere traditions, involves much effort and a deep desire to know the historic Church. It may well be that some of that wrestling will involve substantial debates among those who name Christ, for we cannot come to one mind without honesty and by means of shortcuts. In the end we want not a human-designed religion that comes through calculated compromise and surface fascination with unexplored ideas and practices. The warning of C. S. Lewis uttered in the middle of the last century remains salutary: "It seems to me that the very 'extremist' elements in every church are nearest one another and the liberal and 'broad-minded' people in each Body could never be united at all. . . . The world of 'broad-mindedness' and watered-down 'religion' is a world where a small number of people (all of the same type) say totally different things and change their minds every few minutes. We shall never get re-union from them."[19]

As an Orthodox Christian, I am delighted when those who are new to classic Christian practice, worship, and teaching rediscover an element of the Way that has been obscured or even lost in their own ecclesial tradition—so long as the interest is not merely superficial and so long as the rediscovery is not happily accommodated in an incoherent collection of ideas and practices. Perhaps the best immediate response to this discussion of tradition would be for a dissenting or reforming Christian to turn back to his or her own particular tradition and get to know it better, discovering where and why it varies with the longer traditional patterns of the East and West (not to speak of an analysis of the commonalities and differences—some of the latter substantial—between East and West!). For those who, like me, are members of a community that has declared its allegiance to the Holy Tradition, there are different challenges. One of these will be to humbly acknowledge where the Holy Tradition has come to have only a formal place in the community's life, without really making its mark: in such cases, the Tradition needs to be reclaimed, naturalized and allowed a living place once again. Another challenge will be our generous willingness to differentiate between cherished, but mutable, traditions and Holy Tradition, and not to arrogantly

19. Lewis, "Answers to Questions on Christianity," 60.

join these together so that we put a stumbling block before Christians from other cultural backgrounds who are seeking to understand the eternal and mysterious nature of the Church. The Christian who recently has found a place in the historic Church especially may be tempted to cleave to all things antiquarian, forging a new ecclesial fundamentalism, spending inordinate amounts of time exploring past traditions, and obscuring (with all good intentions) the "one thing necessary" in Holy Tradition.

As Christians continue to discuss these matters, may it be that we are seeking together the mind of Christ so that together we might, through the "Spirit of wisdom and of revelation" come more and more to "know . . . the riches of his glorious inheritance in the saints" and the greatness of "the hope to which he has called" us (Eph. 1:17–19 EH). We may be confident that our LORD, the King of all ages, is not in a hurry. He has ways and means of speaking so that his sheep will hear his voice, so that his "high priestly prayer" for unity in John 17 will be fulfilled. The Church herself, reflecting the vitality of her LORD, may be seen as a sprawling tree, planted by the river of the Spirit: her leaves also do not wither and she prospers. After all, Psalm 1, though it describes most perfectly the fruitfulness of the true Human Being, Jesus, is God's will for his living Church. Yet her unimpeded growth is not automatic, nor does it occur without the consent and participation of the members of the body. As we are directed, "His divine power has bestowed on us everything that makes for life and devotion. . . . We now have the prophetic message made more certain. You will do well to be attentive to it, as to a lamp shining in a dark place, until day dawns and the morning star rises in your hearts" (2 Pet. 1:3, 19 EH). Such attentiveness may take different shapes for different Christians, depending upon where they now find themselves worshiping. It is my hope that all those who name Christ will arrive at a place where they will understand more of the treasure of Holy Tradition given to the Church and have more confidence in articulating this by the light of the apostolic lamp.

Confidence and attentiveness are the twin characteristics to which God's people are called, mirroring our dual stance of sobriety and joy, as we inhabit two worlds—the world that is passing away and the eternal world of God's kingdom that we are even now glimpsing together with gradually transformed eyes. Recognizing and receiving the gift that God has given to us, the gift of himself, illumined by the Scripture and enshrined and expressed in a living Tradition, is the first decisive step into that new world. Then we move beyond a formal recognition of the gift to living it. Understanding and retaining Holy Tradition and negotiating passing traditions are part of living together in the Church: these are not tasks for the confused, for the faint of heart, or for the arrogant.

Today there is a common adage that is often proclaimed without nuance: "Things must change in order to stay the same." This is true, and yet it is also true that "Things must stay the same in order for change to be useful." After all, if everything changes, then there is nothing left! The One who opens our eyes to his truth is that "unchangeable One" in whom there is "no shadow of turning"—yet he *became* Man, assuming humanity for our sake. With God, the essence remains immutable, though he is heartbreakingly responsive to the needs of his own humble creation. It is by him, then, that we can, with prayer and in patience, discern changeable traditions from that abiding and life-giving Tradition to which we have been handed over. To know and accept that which we have received means also to accept the challenge of God's people to read, interpret, inhabit, "apply," and embody God's Word, mindful that this is our work together, with attention to past and present, East and West, and those of high esteem and humbler station. Together, and with our eyes illumined, may we allow the Holy Spirit to show us where the mosaic before us may need to be rearranged because a piece has slipped or been turned in the wrong direction, and to rejoice when the jewels are exactly where they should be because of those who placed them there. So may the great King appear in all his glory before our eyes, and also before the eyes of those who do not yet perceive his splendor. To us "this charge has been handed over. . . . To the King eternal, to the One who is incorruptible and invisible, the only God, be honor and glory unto ages of ages, Amen" (1 Tim. 1:18, 17 EH).

BIBLIOGRAPHY

Abraham, William J. "Scripture, Tradition, and Revelation: An Appreciative Critique of David Brown." Forthcoming in *Theology, Aesthetics, and Culture: Responses to the Work of David Brown*, edited by Robert MacSwain and Taylor Worley. Oxford: Oxford University Press, 2012.

———. "What's Right and What's Wrong with the Quadrilateral?" *Canadian Methodist Historical Society Papers* 13 (2000): 136–50.

Attenborough, F. L., ed. and trans. *The Laws of the Earliest English Kings*. New York: Russell and Russell, 1963.

Barton, John. *Reading the Old Testament: Method in Biblical Study*. Revised and enlarged edition. Louisville: Westminster John Knox, 1996.

Bauckham, Richard J. *Jude and 2 Peter*. Word Commentary 50. Waco: Word, 1983.

———. "Tradition in Relation to Scripture and Reason." In *Scripture, Tradition and Reason: A Study in the Criteria of Christian Doctrine*, edited by Richard J. Bauckham and Benjamin Drewery, 117–45. Edinburgh: T&T Clark, 1988.

Bauckham, Richard J., and Benjamin Drewery, eds. *Scripture, Tradition and Reason: A Case Study in the Criteria of Christian Doctrine*. Edinburgh: T&T Clark, 1988.

Behr, John. *The Way to Nicea*. Formation of Christian Theology I. Crestwood, NY: St. Vladimir's Seminary Press, 2001.

The Book of Alternative Services of the Anglican Church of Canada. Toronto: Anglican Book Centre, 1985.

Breck, John. *Scripture in Tradition: The Bible and Its Interpretation in the Orthodox Church*. Crestwood: St. Vladimir's Seminary Press, 2001.

Brown, David. *Tradition and Imagination: Revelation and Change*. Oxford University Press, 1999.

Brown, Harold O. J. "Proclamation and Preservation: The Necessity and Temptations of Church Traditions." In *Reclaiming the Great Tradition: Evangelicals, Catholics and Orthodox in Dialogue*, edited by James S. Cutsinger, 69–87. Downers Grove, IL: InterVarsity, 1997.

Bruce, F. F. "Scripture in Relation to Tradition and Reason." In *Scripture, Tradition and Reason: A Study in the Criteria of Christian Doctrine*, edited by Richard J. Bauckham and Benjamin Drewery, 35–64. Edinburgh: T&T Clark, 1988.

Clarke, Adam. *Commentary on the Bible*, originally published in eight volumes, 1810–26. http://www.preteristarchive.com/Books/1810_clarke_commentary.html. Accessed January 2012.

Cutsinger, James S., ed. *Reclaiming the Great Tradition: Evangelicals, Catholics and Orthodox in Dialogue*. Downers Grove, IL: InterVarsity, 1997.

Hays, Richard B. *Echoes of Scripture in the Letters of Paul*. New Haven and London: Yale University Press, 1989.

Heid, Stefan. *Celibacy in the Early Church: The Beginnings of a Discipline of Obligatory Continence for Clerics in East and West*. Translated by M. Miller. San Francisco: Ignatius Press, 2001.

Humphrey, Edith M. *Ecstasy and Intimacy: When the Holy Spirit Meets the Human Spirit*. Grand Rapids: Eerdmans, 2005.

———. "Elizabeth Stuart Bowdler." In *Handbook of Women Biblical Interpreters: A Historical and Biographical Guide*, edited by Marion Ann Taylor, 89–93. Grand Rapids: Baker Academic, 2012.

———. "Why Bring the Word Down? The Rhetoric of Demonstration and Disclosure in Romans 9:30–10:13." In *Romans and the People of God: Festschrift for Gordon Fee*, edited by S. Soderlund and N. T. Wright, 129–48. Grand Rapids: Eerdmans, 1999.

———. "Why We Worship God as Father, Son and Holy Spirit." *Crux* 32, no. 2 (1996): 2–12.

Hurtado, Larry W. *Lord Jesus Christ: Devotion to Jesus in Earliest Christianity*. Grand Rapids: Eerdmans, 2005.

Kirk, Alan. "Social and Cultural Memory." In *Memory, Tradition and Text: Uses of the Past in Early Christianity*, edited by Alan Kirk and Tom Thatcher, 1–24. Semeia 52. Atlanta, GA: Society of Biblical Literature, 2005.

Kugel, James L. *Traditions of the Bible: A Guide to the Bible as It Was at the Start of the Common Era*. Cambridge, MA: Harvard, 1998.

Lewis, C. S. "Answers to Questions on Christianity," in *God in the Dock: Essays on Theology and Ethics*, 48–67. Grand Rapids: Eerdmans, 1970.

———. *Reflections on the Psalms*. First edition, 1958; Orlando, FL: Harcourt, 1986.

Lossky, Vladimir. *Orthodox Theology: An Introduction.* Translated by Ian and Ihita Kesarcodi-Watson. Crestwood, NY: St. Vladimir's Seminary Press, 1989.

Lubac, Henri de, SJ. *L'Écriture dans la tradition.* Paris: Aubier Montaigne, 1966.

Melton, Isaac (Fr. Andrew). "A Response to Harold O. J. Brown." In *Reclaiming the Great Tradition: Evangelicals, Catholics and Orthodox in Dialogue,* edited by James S. Cutsinger, 87–99. Downers Grove, IL: InterVarsity, 1997.

Nassif, Bradley. "Will the 21st Be the Orthodox Century?" *Christianity Today,* December 2006. http://www.christianitytoday.com/ct/2006/december/30.40.html. Accessed January 15, 2012.

Newman, John Henry. *The Development of Christian Doctrine.* Westminster, MD: Christian Classics, 1968.

Nouwen, Henri J. M. *Behold the Beauty of the Lord: Praying with Icons.* Notre Dame, IN: Ave Maria Press, 1987.

Outler, Albert, ed. *John Wesley.* New York: Oxford University Press, 1980.

———. "The Wesleyan Quadrilateral in John Wesley." *Wesleyan Theological Journal* 20, no. 1 (Spring 1985): 7–18.

Pelikan, Jaroslav. *The Vindication of Tradition: The 1983 Jefferson Lecture in the Humanities.* New Haven and London: Yale University Press, 1984.

Philokalia: The Complete Text. Compiled by St. Nikodimos of the Holy Mountain and St. Makarios of Corinth and translated from the Greek and edited by G. E. H. Palmer, Philip Sherrard, and Kallistos Ware with the assistance of the Holy Transfiguration Monastery. London: Faber and Faber, 1983.

Ratzinger, Joseph (Pope Benedict XVI). *God's Word: Scripture, Tradition, Office.* Edited by Peter Hünermann and Thomas Söding and translated by Henry Taylor. San Francisco: Ignatius Press, 2008.

Reardon, Patrick Henry. *Christ in the Psalms.* Ben Lomond, CA: Conciliar Press, 2000.

———. "Pastoral Ponderings." *Touchstone* (April 2009). Available online at http://www.allsaintsorthodox.org/pastor/pastoral_ponderings.php. Accessed January 2012.

Stylianopoulos, Theodore G. *The New Testament: An Orthodox Perspective.* Vol. 1. Brookline: Holy Orthodox Press, 1997.

Webber, Robert. "A Call to an Ancient Evangelical Future." *Robert E. Webber Center for an Ancient Evangelical Future* website. http://www.aefcall.org/read.html. Accessed January 2012.

Wright, N. T. *Jesus and the Victory of God.* Minneapolis: Fortress Press, 1996.

———. *What St. Paul Really Said: Was Paul of Tarsus the Real Founder of Christianity?* Grand Rapids: Eerdmans, 1997.

SUBJECT INDEX

Abraham, William, 16, 20
Aland, Kurt, 140n1
Aleichem, Scholem, 2
allegorical reading, 51–52
amanuensis, 70n1
Anabaptists, 8
Ananias, encounter with
     Paul, 102, 130
ancestral traditions, 1, 83
Ancient Christian Commentary on Scripture,
     168n17
angels, 85
Anglican Church of Canada, 169
Anglicans
     "middle position" of,
     11–12
     on tradition, 9
Anglo-Catholics, 12
antitraditionalism, as tradition, 7, 24
apostles, and tradition, 69,
     129–30
Aramaic, 112
Arian conflict, 167
Augustine, 19, 111, 130–31
authorial intent, 166
authorities, in theological
     thinking, 14–15
authority, 89, 91–94, 100,
     103

baptism, 17, 107n4, 154,
     167
*Baptism, Eucharist and
     Ministry*, 169n18
Basil, Saint, 146, 147–48
Bauckham, Richard, 11
Behr, John, 115n2
Benedict XVI, Pope,
     66n22
Bezae text, 140
biblical interpretation,
     162, 163
blessed, 108
blessing God, 109–10
blood of animals, 144–45
Book of Alternative Services (Anglican Church
     of Canada), 169
Bowdler, Susan Stuart,
     39n11
Bowdler, Thomas, 39n11
Breck, John, 80, 163–66
broad-mindedness, 170
Brown, David, 20
Brown, Harold O. J., 10
Bruce, F. F., 63–64
Burke, Edmund, 5–6

"Call to an Ancient Evangelical Future," 10, 20
Calvinists, 19

Canaanite woman, 92
canon, 36, 44, 115
canon of truth, 161, 163
Carlstadt, Andreas, 10
celibacy, 150–52
chain of command, 91,
     101, 134
chain of giving and receiving, 100–101
chastity, 150
checks and balances, in
     early church, 94, 102
cherry-picking, of tradition, 20, 169
Chesterton, G. K., 1
child, recipient of gift as,
     100–102, 108
Childs, B. S., 58n9
Christianity, personal dimension of, 44, 134
Christian liberty, 10
Christology, 117, 164
     and oral tradition, 64
Chrysostom, John, 76,
     151n12
Church, 6
     and biblical interpretation, 163
     change in, 172
     gifts of, 94, 134
     mediation of, 128–30
     relevance of, 88

176

SCRIPTURE INDEX

180